Vampire Culture

Vampire Culture

Maria Mellins

B L O O M S B U R Y

LONDON • NEW DELHI • NEW YORK • SYDNEY

Bloomsbury Academic

An imprint of Bloomsbury Publishing Plc

50 Bedford Square
London
WC1B 3DP
UK

1385 Broadway
New York
NY 10018
USA

www.bloomsbury.com

First published 2013

The material in respect of chapter 1, "Twenty-First-Century Vamp," first appeared
in "The Fangtasia Experience, True Blood Fans, Commodification and Lifestyle"
by Maria Mellins in *TRUE BLOOD: Investigating Vampires and Southern Gothic,*
ed. B. Cherry (IB Tauris, 2012).

British Library Cataloguing-in-Publication Data
A catalogue record for this book is available from the British Library.

ISBN: HB: 978-0-8578-5074-4
PB: 978-0-8578-5075-1

Library of Congress Cataloging-in-Publication Data
A catalog record for this book is available from the Library of Congress.

Typeset by Apex CoVantage, LLC, Madison, WI
Printed and bound in India

Contents

List of Illustrations

Acknowledgments

I would like to acknowledge with gratitude the following: The members of the London Vampyre Group, the Vampyre Connexion, and the London Vampire Meetup Group for taking part in this research and sharing their fascination for vampires. Particular debts of gratitude are owed to Cecile, Jenny, Nancy, Rebecca, Lou, Audrey, and Demondaz for their general help and support. I would like to thank Enlyl's Realm, Izaskun Gonzalez, Angel Lumba, and Jim Nemer for the use of their photographs, and special thanks go to Martin Small for contributing such wonderful images throughout this book. I would also like to thank Dr. Brigid Cherry, Dr. Catherine Spooner, Dr. Caroline Ruddell, and Dr. Paul Hodkinson for their constant guidance and generous feedback that has been so crucial to completing this manuscript. Finally, very special thanks go to my husband, Mike, and son, Dylan, for their unwavering support always, and my family—for their love, understanding, and patience.

Twenty-First-Century Vamp

This feels a bit like what a vampire bar would look like if it were a ride in Disneyworld.

—Sookie Stackhouse, upon entering Fangtasia, *True Blood* 1:4
"Escape from Dragon House"

As we move further into the second decade of the twenty-first century, vampires and wider gothic fiction have been firmly resurrected in popular culture. The return of vampire-like style on the catwalk and the spate of recent vampire books, films, and television programs, such as *Twilight, True Blood*, *Being Human*, and *Let the Right One In* suggest there is pleasure to be found in the consumption of vampire-inspired products. In fact, vampires have become so widespread and accessible that it is now possible to purchase gothic clothes on the high street and tweet-watch the latest episode of your favorite vampire television show with a wider audience of online fans. You can drop into online environments such as Coffin Cafe and contribute to conversations such as, "Do real vampires hate *Twilight*?" and "Why vampires are better than werewolves" as well as visiting real-world vampire-themed architectures, such as Fangtasia London, Bethnal Green's vampire bar.

A sequence from the recent and remarkably popular *True Blood* television series serves as a useful analogy to illustrate just how pervasive vampires have become in popular culture. During season one, Sookie Stackhouse enters Fangtasia bar in Shreveport for the first time. She is immediately met with the sight of its vampire-friendly clientele. The women are wearing a variety of PVC, leather, and lace garments with fishnets, blood red mini tutus, and black, duct-tape nipple pasties. The men wear their hair long and dye it black or blue. Their eyes drip with dark eyeliner, and they wear matching black lipstick. Together, the vampires and "fangbangers" writhe around a bar that is awash with vintage lamps, red wallpaper, and red and black velvet-soft furnishings. A vampire pole dancer, wearing a black PVC bikini and sprayed-on mini shorts, gyrates with phantom speed to the beat of "Don't Fear the Reaper." In the corner, Sookie notices a merchandising desk, where an older couple purchases Fangtasia T-shirts and other branded paraphernalia; she turns to Bill and remarks that Fangtasia "feels a bit like what a vampire bar would look like if it were a ride in Disneyworld" (*True Blood* 1:4). While this fictional sequence quite satirically uses overblown gothic aesthetics to reveal the vampires' manipulation of their own image or brand so that Fangtasia products appeal to and are consumed by humans (or more precisely by fang-bangers), the sequence from *True Blood* also resonates strongly with recent trends in twenty-first-century popular culture, and specifically with the current salability of the vampire.

Amid the current hype circulating around vampires, there exists a small, dedicated group of people who have been celebrating their interests in the vampire since the early 1990s. Whether choosing to wear fangs that are fitted to the teeth, attending events such as Carve Your Own Tombstone and Bloodlust: Anti-Valentines Party, or just snuggling up with a good old vampire novel and a group of friends at Bibliogoth Book Club, vampires are part and parcel of their everyday lives. These people form the London vampire sub-culture, which is made up of the Vampyre Connexion, the London Vampyre Group, and the Vampire Meetup Group, and will be the central focus of this book. Membership to the subculture is diverse and includes people ages six-teen to sixty-five, single, married, straight, bisexual, and gay, from groups of friends to families, from train drivers to university lecturers, from librarians to bankers.

However, before I set about introducing the vampire subculture, "fangs and all," a book that claims to be on the subject of vampire culture must begin by addressing this recent and quite remarkable infiltration of vampires in main-stream popular culture. Therefore, this chapter is a prelude to the main act; it is an overview of contemporary vampire mania. As the title of this book sug-gests, the focus here is concerned with the cultural aspects of the vampire, as opposed to providing detailed analysis of vampire books, films, and televi-sion. Accordingly, I will not restrict this investigation to a mere account of con-temporary fiction but will instead explore the areas that fall outside of these fictions and how people absorb the vampire into their *lifestyle*, from vampire-inspired fashion designs to lifestyle activities, such as vampire-themed bars. What can these creatures of fiction offer in a time of very real social, political, and economic instability?

CATWALK VAMPIRES: FROM FICTION TO FASHION

Historically, the fashion catwalk has been associated with presenting emaciated, beautiful models with hollow stares that stalk the runway in seemingly undead, trancelike states. However, currently the garments that these models wear are equally vampiric in design. While vampire-influenced seasonal trends are certainly not a new phenomenon, and fashion designers have excavated the undead throughout various periods in history,[1] the recent appetite for vampire-styled collections that haunt the past is unparalleled. For instance, the recent Fashion Institute of Technology (FIT) "Gothic: Dark Glamour"[2] exhibition (2008–9) that was organized into themes of Strange Beauty, The Batcave, The Cabinet of Curiosities, and the Ruined Castle, explored how the gothic inspires high fashion. In the book that accompanied the exhibition, Valerie Steele (2008) details the work of recent, influential designers, such as Kei Kagami's monstrous steampunk productions and Alexander McQueen's Voss collection, which conjures images of vampirism, decay, and blood disease. Similarly, Giles Deacon's darkly fetishistic collection for Autumn/Winter 2011–12 is strongly influenced by Victorian and Edwardian designs (Blank 2011), and the recent *ASOS* magazine article "The Edge of Darkness" also charts designers such as Wunderkind's strong-shouldered dresses and exaggerated silhouettes, Nina Ricci's Tuxedo jackets, and the Mulleavy sisters of Rodarte's "Frankenstein's monster-inspired take on the Gothic" as being influential contributions to the "*Twilight* Effect" (Magdalino 2009: 76).

Fashion on the high street has consequently adopted a deathly aesthetic, with a Victorian edge. Recent seasons' trends have included an array of lace, leather, and velvet fabrics and tailored tops, dresses, and coats with sharply architectured shoulders and Victorian necklines. Shoes and boots are chunky and loose around the ankle, making legs look thin and fragile; even stilettos must be extreme. The cosmetics industry also demonstrates how vampire narratives and archetypes are used to market products. Popular cosmetics include deep plum and burgundy lip color, worn with pallid complexions, starkly contrasted with soft, damson, pinched cheeks and long, dark, dramatic, spidery eyelashes. This is all framed by messy, backcombed, texturized hair, creating the overall look of a beautifully tragic porcelain doll. For instance, the Illamasqua brand, "makeup for your alter ego," playfully referenced a sequence from Francis Ford Coppola's *Bram Stoker's Dracula* for their Sirens range.[3] The campaign includes photographs of two attractive, scantily clad young women, wearing gold, swirling headbands; their skin has a shimmering blue, cyanosis tinge. They are writhing around on a stone background, seducing a bare-chested, dark-haired man. The scene pays homage to a sequence in the film where Jonathan Harker (Keanu Reeves) is seduced by the devil's concubines.

As these examples from the fashion and beauty industry demonstrate, in mainstream culture, the vampire now provides pleasure-seeking opportunities. As Sookie's remark about Disneyland in the epigraph reveals, instead of representing purely evil beings, contemporary vampires—similar to the spectacle of a theme park ride—now symbolize a certain playfulness. Or, as Catherine Spooner asserts, in her discussion of twenty-first-century gothic, these vampires exhibit a "new lightness" that invites us to revel in "sensation" and "entertainment," as we now have a celebratory attitude towards the gothic, or what might be termed "Happy Goth" (Spooner 2009: 1). Although vampire clothes and accessories evoke a sense of drama and edginess (i.e., usually associated with subcultural dress), the fact that you can pick up vampire clothes and accessories in shops such as Topshop and Zara clearly demonstrates that vampires and wider gothic culture are now "witty, sexy, cool" (Spooner 2010: xi).

Returning to the analogy between vampires and Disneyworld, the vampire is not only associated with pleasure-seeking opportunities but is also linked with wider merchandising and commodification parallels. Much like Disney World's recent addition of The Wizarding World of Harry Potter, with rides such as Hogwarts Forbidden Journey and Flight of the Hippogriff, it is not difficult to imagine how fictions penned by Stephenie Meyer, Charlaine Harris, and L. J. Smith could be easily transformed into distinct, vampire-themed worlds such as Mystic Falls, Forks, and Bon Temps, with teenagers screaming on rides named The Doppelganger, inspired by *Vampire Dairies*, or Leap of Faith, in the style of Bella's cliff dive in *New Moon*, while their parents settle down to a meal at Merlotte's. Although these specific market synergies have yet to be realized, recent vampire fictions have diversified into a multitude of wider consumer areas. Like their predecessors *Buffy the Vampire Slayer* and *Angel*, recent vampire texts such as *Twilight* and *True Blood* possess complex, world-making potentials that can be mined by the industry as well as by viewers of the show (Jenkins 2008).[4] While this does not extend to all recent vampire texts in the same way (e.g., *Let the Right One In* does not share merchandising potentials to the same extent), our relationship with the vampire in the twenty-first century is—now more than ever—a commodified experience. In order to understand how vampires are increasingly being transformed into commodities and absorbed into lifestyle activities, this discussion will now investigate a popular, contemporary vampire franchise in detail.

TRUE BLOOD CASE STUDY: VAMPIRE COMMODIFICATION AND LIFESTYLE

True Blood contains a visual, encyclopedic universe that can be mined by viewers of the show. For instance, both the novels and the television show place a strong emphasis on dress. Similar to Charlaine Harris's *Aurora Teagarden Series*, the *Southern Vampire Mysteries* are littered with superfluous detail about Sookie's latest outfits, hairstyles, and cosmetics. The *True Blood* series's costume designers also carefully construct a very specific image for Sookie, with her natural, fresh-faced makeup, long blond hair, floral dresses, and array of tiny shorts that constantly expose her perfect tan. Sookie's clothes and accessories throughout the series present her—in sharp contrast to the vampires—as a character that is happier outdoors; she is a distinctly southern sun worshipper, with an ethereal quality (which is a hint toward her fae heritage). In addition to containing excessive details concerning dress, the *True Blood* universe also includes easily identifiable, branded architectures such as Fangtasia, Merlotte's Bar & Grill, and Lou Pines. These familiar architectures can then be mined and excavated by both HBO and fans of the franchise.

From even the most cursory of glances at HBO's *True Blood* website[5] it is possible to note how the stylistic features of the *True Blood* universe have diversified into wider media. There are a range of branded *True Blood* commodities offered, including Merlotte's Bar & Grill waitress uniforms with matching apron; apparel from the vampire-rights group, the American Vampire League; Bon Temps varsity jackets, in the style of Jason Stackhouse; Herveaux Contracting baseball caps, based on those fashioned by Alcide Herveaux in the third season; Fangtasia neon signs; Type O-Negative Tru:Blood drink sets; and T-shirts from the Lou Pines Packmaster's Were Bar. Fans can purchase products printed with quotable references to the *True Blood* universe, such as T-shirts printed with Bill's catchphrase, Sookie is Mine, Team Bill and Team Eric tops, and products with less overt branding, such as Eric's silver bullet necklace. In addition to the official merchandise, there is a whole host of *True Blood* unofficial commodities available on sites such as Etsy[6] and Zazzle.[7] Products include bumper stickers printed with quotes from characters, such as Eric's "Is there blood in my hair?"; Lafayette aprons; Lorena-inspired black resin rose rings; "Bite Me" badges; "I wanna be Sookie" pendants; and hand-painted, wooden baby vampire dolls in the style of characters from the show.

The stylistic features of the show are also reimagined even further, through the organization of an entire lifestyle space—Fangtasia London. Fangtasia London describes itself as "a unique performance club experience with drinking, dancing, and death in the swamplands of Bethnal Green. . . . It's the place to be for vamps, tramps, shape-shifters, were-folk, fangbangers and anyone with a taste for the dark side of the South."[8] Like the HBO series, Fangtasia London does not shy away from the gratuitous edginess of vampire appeal. The venue for the event is the Resistance Gallery, which is located in Poyser Street, a dark and dingy alleyway surrounded by abandoned warehouses and studio space. Unlike the neon sign outside HBO's Fangtasia, there are no external signifiers to herald one's arrival at this real-life event. Instead, visitors must knock on the steel shutter and be invited in. The unwieldiness of the venue immediately creates a sense of tension for newcomers, as they must cross the threshold without any idea of what they might find on the other side.

Upon entering the Resistance Gallery, the familiarity of the *True Blood* universe is apparent. The space contains familiar furniture from HBO's Fangtasia—the bar is lined with bottles of Type O-Negative Tru:Blood, and upstairs patrons have the opportunity to purchase imitation vampire fangs, custom fitted to their own teeth by Blood Red FX. Death country, southern rock, grunge, goth, and metal blare out from two large speakers. A stage has been erected that contains a dancing pole, a bloodred curtain (that masks the entrance for the performance acts), a wooden stand with taxidermy objects, and a dilapidated sofa (similar to Eric's throne), where patrons can be photographed in their finest *True Blood* regalia. The event even has its very own Sheriff of E2, as Resistance Gallery CEO and resident DJ Gary Vanderhorne's appearance and presence is a playful homage to the *True Blood* character of Eric Northman, Vampire Sheriff of Area 5. Not surprisingly, dressing up is an important part of the event, and patrons fashion a diverse range of ensembles, from American Deep South–inspired outfits to wider gothic vampire clothes and accessories.

As the case study of *True Blood* demonstrates, like gothic-inspired fashion that is currently popular on the high street, Fangtasia London is also associated with identity factors and pleasure-seeking opportunities; the event allows people to enjoy experiences outside of the ordinary and engage in alternative lifestyles. So, returning to the question posed at the beginning of this chapter, concerning what the vampire has to offer in the twenty-first century, Peter Ingwersen, the fashion designer and founder of the fashion label Bllack Noir, offers a potential response. Ingwersen attributes the increased fascination with vampires to a wider sense of boredom, or lack, in contemporary culture, as there is now "a real need to look into alternative worlds. Our taste for the gothic is increasing with its tales of drama, fairytales and dark powers. Everything a reality show cannot give you" (Ingwersen, in Magdalino 2009: 76). So, while the possibility of vampires, werewolves, shape shifters, fairies, and humans coexisting together does not necessarily make for idyllic social and political harmony (many sequences with the American Vampire Alliance and the Fellowship of the Sun are evidence of that), the *True Blood* universe, like wider vampire fiction and fashion, offers

Figure 1   Image from Fangtasia London advertisement. Photograph: Izaskun Gonzalez. Model: Kate Lomax

fascinating potentials for a more interesting, sexy, and cool way of life. Essentially, our relationship with the vampire has changed; instead of resembling evil or amoral forces, vampires now offer us more interesting and even desirable futures.

VAMPIRE CULTURE

This chapter has demonstrated that the vampire assumes a prized and privileged position in twenty-first-century popular culture. However, while these examples of contemporary vampire fascination are useful in demonstrating the widespread popularity and profitability of vampires, this chapter has only just begun to explore the potentials of vampire lifestyle. In order to gain a deep and significant insight into vampire culture and, specifically, issues of gender, fashion, and fandom, an ethnographic investigation into vampire subculture is warranted. Using data that have been collected from the London-based vampire community, including questionnaires, in-depth interviews, and online and face-to-face participant observations, this book presents a snapshot of the vampire subculture and how it exists in the UK today.

Before I move on to introduce the vampire subculture in detail, I must first clarify a few decisions that I have made that have implications on this study. First, I must account for the terminology I have used. I will be using the terms *community* and *subculture* interchangeably throughout this book. *Community* is quite a straightforward term, as it is used by participants when describing themselves (i.e., We are a community of people who love all things vampire), whereas the term *subculture* is somewhat more complex, as it is steeped with a variety of academic implications dating back to the Chicago School of Sociology (see Cressey 1932; Gordon 1947; A. K. Cohen 1955/1997) and the Centre for Contemporary Cultural Studies (CCCS) at Birmingham University in the 1970s. Like Dunja Brill (2008), who draws on the work of Paul Hodkinson (2002) in her book *Goth Culture*, I have also experienced difficulties in attempting to find a suitable label for a group of real people that all have very different experiences and lives. Therefore, I will also be drawing on Hodkinson's new definition of subculture that, as Brill suggests, moves away from previous connotations of youth, the working classes, deviancy, and collective resistance (Brill 2008: 25) and instead focuses on the substance of the subculture and recognizes that "even the most substantive of subcultures will retain elements of diversity . . . and that even the most committed participants are not somehow isolated from other interests and priorities" (Hodkinson 2002: 33).

Also with regard to terminology—although I refer to the London-based vampire community throughout this book, it is important to acknowledge that the community far exceeds the London area. Members travel nationally and internationally to wider vampire-related destinations, including Whitby Goth Weekend (the biannual, large-scale goth festival held in Whitby, North Yorkshire), Leipzig's Wave-Gotik Treffen (the German alternative festival), and Transylvania (the fictional setting for Bram Stoker's *Dracula*). In addition, not all members of the London vampire community live in the capital; some members commute from Hull and Llansannan in Wales, and on occasion members from vampire groups abroad have attended the London scene when traveling to the UK on holiday or business. That being said, the majority of vampire community venues that will be discussed are based in London. The most popular of these include the Devonshire Arms (one of London's most renowned alterative bars, based in Camden, which has a strict, alternative dress policy), the Intrepid Fox (an alternative goth, rock, and punk music pub, and the London Vampyre Group's monthly venue), and the Blue Posts (a pub in Piccadilly that is not particularly linked with the alterative scene but rents an upstairs private room to the Vampyre Connexion on the last Thursday of the month).

Second, as well as clarifying my terminology, I must also explain why this research is so focused on ascertaining how members of the vampire community dress. The preoccupation with vampire clothing and accessories was not the original aim of this study. The research originated as a much more traditional fan study that would explore female fans of vampire media and the text/viewer relationship. It aspired to investigate how members of fan groups engage with vampire television and films, and how they articulate their fanatical interests to other members of the fan community in face-to-face and online contexts. Yet, after meeting the vampire community for the first time in 2007, I realized that vampire *lifestyle* was the truly important consideration, particularly vampire-inspired clothes and commodities. Having just read Matt Hills's book *Fan Cultures*, in which he calls for more exhaustive investigations of dress and costuming within fan studies, because "the site of the body has been largely neglected in previous work on fan cultures" (Hills 2002: 158), I decided that this book must focus on the crucial, often overlooked subject of dress. Dress is defined by Joanne Eicher as "an assemblage of body modifications and/or supplements displayed by a person in communicating with other human beings" (Eicher and Roach Higgins 1992: 15). As this definition establishes, studies into dress must incorporate both the supplements being presented (i.e., vampire garments, jewelry, and accessories) and the social framework in which these modifications are performed. Consequently, throughout this book I will present a detailed description of women's dress practices and what is being communicated to other human beings inside and outside the vampire community's social circle.

Finally, I must account for the gender focus of this research. Although there are some male members of the community, this book will focus on the female members, who make up the largest portion of this group. While I have researched the experiences of male members of the group in some detail, my decision to focus on the female participants was made for several reasons. This was in part due to the comparatively high level of women participating within the community at the time of this research. I made a conscious decision to let the data lead the research so that I could observe what was naturally occurring as opposed to imposing my own ideas on the data, which could potentially skew my findings. The gender focus was also because, unlike other fan communities, such as the female fans of cult media discussed by Joanne Hollows, who position themselves as "one of the boys" (Thornton 1995, in Hollows 2003: 35), the vampire community allows women to respond to their fandom in particularly *feminine* ways, such as hairstyling, shopping, and creating their own vampire-inspired jewelry, clothes, and accessories. I noticed interesting negotiations of femininity occurring within the community that were worthy of closer inspection. On a more personal level, I also felt that the vampire had always held a strong appeal for women, with the popularity of vampire fiction dating back to the early nineteenth century and to the six-penny blue books that were particularly associated with a young, lower-class female readership (as discussed by Williamson 2005). As a woman and a vampire fan, I wanted to understand this relationship in more detail.

Therefore, in the next six chapters, the overarching theme of the book is concerned with how female members of the vampire community draw on and commodify the legend of the vampire in their everyday life. In order to understand the relationship between women and their vampires, I pose four research questions, which are fully documented in chapter 3. These questions are concerned with ascertaining the specific vampire commodities fashioned by members; the gendered discourses that arise; how subcultural status is bestowed; and the antagonisms, tensions, and contradictory experiences that occur within the vampire community.

The following chapter functions as an introduction to me as a researcher and to some of the key members of the vampire community. It briefly outlines my methodology and the research design that informs this analysis. Chapter 3 draws on previously conducted research on subcultures and fan communities and explores the specifically feminine pleasures of vampire community lifestyle and status. It culminates in four research questions that will be asked throughout the book. Having identified the methods and previous literature that are of use to this study, the remaining three chapters will then present the major findings of the research. For the sake of clarity, and in order to gain a rich and full insight into the vampire community, in the final chapters I adopt a journalistic approach and establish the *who*, *what*, *where*, *when*, *how*, and *why* of vampire culture.

Chapter 4, "Vampire Community Profile," uses graphs and photographs to account for the first four of these questions: I offer a descriptive analysis of the community that outlines *who* the vampire community are, *what* vampire lifestyle is, and precisely *where* and *when* these activities (that are almost invisible to wider society) take place. The major areas that will be covered in chapter 4 include vampire community membership, dress and commodities, and vampire fiction. Chapter 5, "Feminine Discourses," accounts for women's motivation for signing up for vampire community membership. This chapter addresses the varied and contradictory identities of women and asks *why* women choose to adorn themselves in clothing and lifestyle accessories that reimagine the past. The discussion identifies four specific discourses, which include the romanticization of the past, excessive femininity, androgyny and variation, and identification and outsiderdom.

Chapter 6, "Alternative Celebrity," presents a case study analysis of the Vampyre Connexion's social secretary, MorbidFrog, a particularly high-profile member of the community. This chapter is a case study of *how* vampire lifestyle is achieved. In a micro sense, it provides rich data of MorbidFrog's daily activities within the vampire community, from her proficient use of online social media to her elaborate style at face-to-face events, which has led to her rich subcultural status and celebrification. This chapter then reflects on wider community politics and demonstrates that although the community may contain style leaders such as MorbidFrog, it also contains those who feel left out of the community and exist on its outskirts because the community is subject to cliques, hierarchies, and fragmentation. The final chapter will then present the major conclusions of this research and highlight the significance of this book. I argue that this research far exceeds a monograph of a single fan community; it is actually a study of how fan communities and subcultures are changing in entity.

−2−

Interviewing Vampires

The location is a flat in Old Street, East London, on a chilly October eve-ning; the event is a fang-fitting party (a social gathering where members get custom-made fangs fitted to their teeth). Those present are me, fangsmith Robbie,[1] and a sprinkling of London Vampyre Group members, including Rebecca, Lou, Nancy, Tina, and Paul. While waiting for our appointments in the dentist chair, we gather in Robbie's living room and happily tuck into a bottle of red wine. Lou flicks through *Gothic Beauty* magazine, which sparks conversations about Emily Autumn, the Victorian Industrialist performance artist who is featured inside. We swap stories about this evening's journey to East London, which include anecdotes about how awkward it is to run for the train when wearing a corset, and some of the offensive remarks encountered en route in response to the group's vampire-styled attire (which is actually rather tame on this Wednesday evening because most people have arrived directly from work).

Conversations usually flow very easily on nights out with the vampire community, but tonight's exchanges were somewhat more stifled because those who had already sat in Robbie's dentistry chair were temporarily in-capacitated. Although the fang-fitting process is entirely painless, once the imitation fangs have been shaped and fitted to the teeth the fangs then need to cool, so that they can fit snugly. New fang wearers have to undergo a short cooling process that involves holding their mouths open while ap-plying pressure to the fangs for ten to fifteen minutes, which renders them speechless, drinkless, and the most they can muster in these awkward moments is to avoid dribbling. Nevertheless, the end product is very realis-tic—two single, high-quality, elongated canine fangs (known as the classic) or lateral incisors (known as the Lilith) that can be popped in and out at a moment's notice.

As I took in the scene, I could not help but smile at my own feelings of ordinariness and comfort during this entirely extraordinary evening. I found myself thinking how my life had transformed. Here I was at a fang-fitting party, with a group of vampire community members, laughing, joking, and chatting about last year's Whitby Goth Weekend festival and Dita Von Teese's latest outfit, while queuing to get custom-made vampire fangs. My social activities before this research had been comparatively less interesting. Outwardly, I have always been rather conventional. Apart from a short phase in the early 1990s—when I was particularly inspired by Madonna and Danni Minogue's rebellious punk character in *Home and Away*, which led to a very temporary but nevertheless quite substantial wardrobe overhaul—I have always dressed in accordance with mainstream fashion. Also, prior to this research I did not have any friends who dressed in alternative clothes or were particularly involved in alternative lifestyle.[2] I had friends who enjoyed vampire fiction, but this only extended to the occasional cinema screening or our sharing of vampire novels. Therefore, in terms of dress and lifestyle, when I began this research I was very much an outsider of the community.

In contrast to my fashion choices, my fictional tastes and interests are more closely aligned with the community, because I am also a fan of vampires and horror fiction and therefore have insights into the field. I grew up reading Point Horror teen-fiction novels, such as *Trick or Treat* and *The Return of the Vampire*; then, during my late teens and early twenties, I became increasingly fascinated with horror and the gothic. It was at this time that I began to infuse my lifestyle with my fanatical interests, surrounding myself with various signifiers, which demonstrated my passion for horror to others. I repeatedly watched horror films, such as *Halloween*, *A Nightmare on Elm Street*, *Scream*, and *I Know What You Did Last Summer* and collected cult commodities such as *Child's Play*, *Alien*, and *Bram Stoker's Dracula*–inspired figurines and T-shirts. I subscribed to horror fanzines *Shivers* and *Fangoria* and attended science fiction/fantasy conventions, such as Collectormania, in order to hear talks by cult stars Robert Englund (Freddy Krueger) and Nicholas Brendon (Xander, in *Buffy the Vampire Slayer*). I also visited geographies that were associated with the gothic, organizing trips to Transylvania, Bram Stoker's fictional setting of *Dracula*, and the Villa Diodati in Lake Geneva, the location where Mary Shelley (accompanied by Lord Byron, Percy Shelley, and John Polidori) conceived *Frankenstein*. At the age of twenty-four I then embarked on this research project, which has allowed me to research vampires and their fans on a full-time basis.

As these examples therefore demonstrate, although I do not dress in alternative fashion in everyday life and tend to prefer pink to black, I do have a fascination with vampires and wider gothic media, and for this reason I refer to my research position throughout this book as a partial insider. As this chapter will document, the partiality of my position had implications on access to the community and has indeed changed over the course of this research, which has provided some fascinating moments. I have encountered acceptance,

but also distrust. I have experienced moments of embarrassment and resistance, but also warmth and encouragement. Above all, I have gained a deep
insight into an extraordinary, articulate, diverse, and virtually invisible subculture. It is the aim of this chapter to fully introduce myself and the subculture,
and to outline the methods I have used to conduct this ethnography. First,
however, I will start from the beginning and explain how I came to research
the London vampire community in the first place.

LOCATING THE COMMUNITY: SORTING THE SANGUINARIANS FROM THE STYLERS

As I mentioned previously, part of my motivation for conducting a research
project into vampire culture was due to my own interests in horror and, more
specifically, vampire fiction. I wondered just what it was about horror and the
vampire that fascinated me to this degree, and just as important, why did I
desire to present my fandom in this way to others? At this stage I did not
have clear answers to these questions, but I knew that in part my interests
were associated with a taste for gothic aesthetics and a morbid curiosity that
went back to childhood. I also aligned my interests with my gender and felt
that there was a level of boundary breaking occurring because I delighted in
subject matter that was not typically associated with women. I enjoyed the
response my fandom met from others, which often included shock and sur-
prise and the suggestion that my tastes were masculine or, at the very least,
similar to those associated with an adolescent boy (even though recent academic work on female pleasures of horror/gothic fiction suggests much to
the contrary; see Cherry 2001).

I knew that these outward signs of identity (purchasing cult commodities
and visiting cult geographies) were crucial to how I wanted to be viewed by
others and how I understood myself. Therefore, after much deliberation, I con-
cluded that my own fandom was bound up with issues of gender and, more
specifically, with femininity and identity. My fandom did not meet such a surprised response from others because of my sex (i.e., having an XX chromo-
some as opposed to an XY) but rather because my tastes in horror, gore, and
violence were at odds with the cultural construction of what it means to be
female, or feminine. At this stage, such insights into my own fan experiences
were purely hypothetical; I needed to locate a wider sample of vampire fans
to further investigate issues of gender and identity.

Consequently, I began to familiarize myself with several vampire communities that were operating in the UK. I came across two groups—the Dark

Souls of Nottingham and the Manchester Vampire Meetup Group—that contained some suitable participants. However, the Dark Souls were more focused on general gothic pleasures as opposed to being specifically attached to the vampire, and the Manchester group contained members who were self-proclaimed real vampires in the form of blood fetishists and psychic vampires, or energy vamps, and therefore I felt they would distract attention from the cultural focus of this study. Similarly, I was not convinced about members' commitment to these groups, and both groups have since ceased to exist, typical of the short-term nature of many of these communities. Therefore, I disregarded these groups and located vampire fan groups in Northampton, Brighton, and London. Out of these groups, the London scene was extremely well established and would serve as the most useful case study. It had many loyal members, and its location in England's busy capital meant that there was a high level of activity to observe.

I began to conduct some initial background research into the London vampire community, which raised as many questions as it answered. First, I learned that the community was not a sanguinarian organization and did not believe in the existence of so-called real vampires. The FAQ's section on the London Vampyre Group's website states that "we are not a contact organisation for anyone seeking blood drinkers and we do not exist to encourage such activities . . . the vampire is a fantasy figure who exists only in the fictional imagination" (LVG website). Second, from the photographs in the respective vampire community fanzines and websites, I noticed that the community contained a high proportion of women and that they were extremely engaged with lifestyle activities and with fashioning a pseudo-historical vampire style. Photographs documented them in a range of settings, from posing on graveyard walks at Nunhead Cemetery to drinking and chatting as they took part in a vampire pub quiz. In each scenario they wore outfits comprising corsets as outerwear and black lace and velvet bustled skirts that trailed the floor. Outfits were accessorized with fangs, black parasols, elaborate makeup, silver jewelry, and predominantly dark or red hair.

These fashion and lifestyle activities simultaneously fascinated and puzzled me. I knew that the community was not a blood-cultist community, but I also suspected from members' dress practices that it was not just about reading vampire books and watching vampire films. While I was sure that the community must include fans of vampire fiction like myself (the website also contained reviews of vampire novels, television, and wider media), these photographs revealed that the vampire community also appeared to offer members a vampire lifestyle and a social culture.

I wondered what driving forces were behind vampire community member-ship and what compelled people to join a group that was so devoted to vampires that they wore their fascinations on their bodies. Were these vampire costumes worn only for vampire events, or were these clothes part of their daily wardrobe?

The large number of women within the community also presented po-tentially interesting lines of inquiry concerning gender identity. From the garments women wore in the photographs, it was evident that alternative negotiations of femininity were occurring here. Like my own consumption of vampire media that centered around subtle rejections or, at the very least, resistance to cultural constructions of femininity, these women were going further and donning entire sartorial identities that were at odds with socially sanctioned forms of dress. I wanted to understand more about vampire fash-ion and what women's attitudes to vampire lifestyle accessories revealed about their experiences of modern femininity. I decided that in order to shed some light on these dress and lifestyle factors, I must research the origins of the London vampire community and how it fits in with wider subcultures, such as goths.

VAMPIRES AND LONDON'S ALTERNATIVES

It is useful to briefly introduce some of the wider subcultures in which vam-pire members coexist and interact because there is often a high degree of crossover among London's alternative scenes.[3] First and most recently, vam-pire members draw on the emerging steampunk subculture for inspiration in their dress practices (see chapter 5). Steampunk is a literary genre that has recently evolved as a subcultural constructor of identity. Steampunk, as the name suggests, is an anachronistic movement that reimagines a his-torical, predominantly Victorian fantasy (harking back to a time of steam power), which is then fused or "punked" with futuristic science and technol-ogy. BDSM[4] and fetish communities also coexist with the vampire community. London's fetishists gather at events such as Torture Garden, which describes itself on its website as the largest fetish/body art club. Participants dress in highly sexualized clothing, including rubber, PVC, spandex, and leather mate-rials, which are also evident among styles worn by the vampire community. Fetish garments adopted by vampire members include PVC corsets and knee-high boots, and both groups often engage in piercings and body art. Finally, and most predominantly, there is also a strong goth subculture operating in London. In his book *Street Style*, Ted Polhemus identifies goth as a profusion of black velvets, lace fishnets and leather tinged with scarlet or purple, accessorized with tightly laced corsets, gloves, precarious stilettos and silver jewellery depicting religious and occult themes. Hair was jet black, back-combed to reach the stars. Faces were pancaked to deathly white with eyes and lips slashed with blood-red or black. (1994: 97)

As Polhemus's description of goth appearance demonstrates, there are strong similarities between the goth subculture and the London vampire community. For instance, both groups draw on a shared visual language. They favor black and construct an identity that hinges on a morbid, often historical reimagining of the past. Members from goth and vampire communities also attend similar events and may find themselves rubbing shoulders at popular alternative venues and festivals, such as Whitby Goth Weekend. However, although these two groups share interlocked histories, they are by no means the same subculture.

The similarities between these groups go back to the early 1990s, when the London vampire community first began. In *Goth* (2002), Paul Hodkinson explores the origins of the goth style and suggests that music and performance artists such as David Bowie, Joy Division, Siouxsie and the Banshees, The Cure, Bauhaus (most notably, the single *Bela Lugosi's Dead*), and the Leeds group The Sisters of Mercy, all contributed to the emergence of the stylistic characteristics of goth (2002: 36). Crucially, Hodkinson notes that as goth style evolved into the 1990s, there was a "more direct link between goth participants and vampire fiction" (2002: 46) as horror, and particularly vampire film iconography such as crosses, fake blood, and, in some cases, imitation fangs began to be used in gothic outfits. Films such as *Bram Stoker's Dracula* also resulted in a renewed enthusiasm for historical period clothing, such as corsets, lace, and bustled skirts (Hodkinson 2002: 46). This link between gothic style and vampire iconography was particularly noticeable among a small subdivision of the community, as Hodkinson points out:

Among a somewhat smaller minority, particularly taken by the vampire theme, status-bestowing personal decorations also came to include fake fangs, coloured contact lenses and elaborate "horror" style make-up. Indeed there was something of a loosely bounded subgroup, in which a direct emphasis on vampire fiction—via appearance, conversations, collections of literature, and even role-playing games—was particularly noticeable. (2002: 46)

At approximately the same time that vampire iconography was gaining popularity on the goth scene, the first vampire community was set up in London, known as the Vampyre Society—which later splintered into two groups: the London Vampyre Group (LVG) and the Vampyre Connexion (VC); more recently, the London Vampire Meetup Group (LVMG) has also opened its doors. Due to the goth scene's mounting appetite for vampires at this time, a number of goths joined the Vampyre Society. Therefore, in light of these links, the vampire community's tendency to fashion an alternative vampire style is only to be expected. However, the vampire community is far more complex than merely existing as a simple offshoot of the goth subculture. The vampire community may have historical ties to the goth scene, but unlike goths, who tend to be much more strongly associated with music and identity subculture, the vampire community contains both people who engage in subcultural practices and fans of the genre who do not to the same extent align their interests with dress.

In contrast to goths, the London vampire community exists as a community for people who have a specific fascination with *vampires*, as opposed to the general gothic. It provides the opportunity to attend eclectic, vampire-themed events, but in general the community is less concerned with music and gig nights. Like goth subculture, the vampire community provides a space for people to engage in a level of subcultural dress, but the outfits fashioned at vampire events draw on a rather specific version of morbid femininity. Although variations do exist, the majority of women prefer a specifically historical and romantic style of clothing. They rarely wear modern styles of alterative dress (such as cybergoth) for vampire nights but instead present a *Vicwardian* femininity, a term used by vampire members to describe the fusion of Victorian and Edwardian styles, wearing garments comprising bustled skirts, corsets, antique lace, and, of course, fangs.

This hybrid nature of the London vampire community, with *both* its strong links to subcultural lifestyle (particularly those associated with vampire styles of dress) and its loose attraction to a shared beloved text (i.e., it contains fans of vampire media) has major implications on this research. Thus far, work on fan cultures had been split into two categories—the work on fans (i.e., Jenkins 1992 and others) and the work on music and youth subcultures (i.e., Hebdige 1979 and others). As Hills suggests in *Fan Cultures*, this has led to specific and rather narrow dimensions of "the fan" (2002: 65). Conducting research into the vampire community, which blurs the boundary between fans and subcultures, provides the opportunity to investigate how these two areas might be reframed and brought together to widen the parameters of fan research. This book is therefore primarily concerned with investigating vampire culture and how the vampire is drawn upon, consumed, commodified, and accessorized within people's lifestyle. By acknowledging these external lifestyle factors within the vampire community, this book paves the way for future studies into fans' relationship with media texts and the performative pleasures that are occurring.

STAKING (OUT) VAMPIRES: ACCESS AND TRUST

In order to investigate vampire culture and lifestyle, it was essential to capture data on all aspects of community members' day-to-day activities. The best way to do this was to enter the field myself and become thoroughly involved in community life. In *Tales of the Field: On Writing Ethnography* (1988), key ethnographer John Van Maanen describes ethnography as full-time, extremely demanding fieldwork that usually involves living alongside the members of the culture or subculture being studied. Throughout this research I have predominantly used ethnographic research techniques because I have immersed myself in vampire culture since 2007. I have conducted in-depth group and individual interviews[5] with fifteen members of the community (who were also tracked online) and documented my own observations at various lifestyle contexts in a research diary. I have also drawn on case study analysis of eight female members and distributed questionnaires[6] to just under 50 percent of the community.[7] Heeding Sarah Thornton's advice, that media consumption is a vital area to investigate when exploring subcultures, and particularly when addressing questions of status and cultural distinction (Thornton 1995: 203); I also interrogated the media that circulated the community, including *Chronicles* fanzine (the London Vampyre Group publication) and *Dark Nights* (the Vampyre Connexion publication).

Although the majority of this research is based on data collected through ethnographic methods,[8] I have also captured some quantitative data that is not traditionally associated with ethnography (see chapter 4). I made the decision to capture quantitative data so that I could shed light on the types of people who made up the vampire community. I designed the questionnaire to capture some basic demographic information, which provided me with various statistical and descriptive details about the community, including education, employment, sexuality, and nationality, which could then be built upon in more detail during the analysis of my ethnographic findings.

My decision to employ an ethnographic approach has allowed me to enter the deeper workings of the vampire community and become privy to inside information, yet my journey to this point has not been straightforward. Going back to the fang-fitting party discussed at the beginning of this chapter, the feelings of comfort and acceptance that I experienced that evening were certainly not representative of all my exchanges with the vampire community. Initially, there were problems with trust and gaining access. Members of the vampire community have had to develop thick skins and become rather guarded. From the outset there were obvious cliques and friendships that made it extremely difficult to find an opening. The situation was exacerbated by my decision to continue to wear items from my usual wardrobe to the majority of events, which signaled my difference and solidified my position as an outsider.

From my first night out on the vampire scene, in January 2007 (which was an LVG monthly meeting that took place in a private room at the Intrepid Fox), I had to think very carefully about my clothes and accessories and how I wanted to present myself to the community. As a researcher I felt that I needed to be as honest as possible and felt that dressing up would have ethical repercussions on this study, because on some level I would be conducting covert research. From my observations of the vampire community websites, I was extremely aware of the community's reservations about researchers. These reservations were largely in response to the previous exploitation that the community had incurred, as journalist's reports have included references to blood drinking and general misrepresentation and ridicule of the community. I also later realized that the community was particularly sensitive to outsiders due to the prejudicial treatment and abuse that had been incurred. This ranged from being heckled in the street with taunts, such as "Marilyn Manson," to much more alarming, violent outbursts. One participant discussed how she had a bottle thrown at her head and also narrowly escaped quite literally being set on fire outside a nightclub, on account of her being a witch.

> MorbidFrog: I get hassle all the time, people shout "goth," "freak." People have thrown bottles at me on the night bus for just being alternative. I was outside a club and someone decided I was a witch. I was really scared they were going to set me on fire. I had to get security. Sometimes when I go out I deliberately wear a scarf and a hood; I don't try to hide, but I don't want to get too noticed either. (Individual Interview 3)

I also found myself on the receiving end of this treatment on more than one occasion, although to a much lesser extent. For instance, my selection of red wine at the bar during a London Vampyre Group monthly meeting resulted in a number of sniggers and snide remarks about blood drinking.[9]

Going back to my first night out with the vampire community, and my quandary about how I was going to present myself, I felt that these insider/

outsider tensions were a real issue that I needed to counter. I tried to find the balance between being myself and not dressing in a manner that might be deemed antagonistic or hostile to people in the community. I finally settled on wearing darker clothes than usual but chose garments (a black skirt and charcoal gray T-shirt) that were deliberately nondescript and would not be conceived as alternative. Initially, my decision to not dress like the rest of the community did delay my access and proved embarrassing at times, but as I continued to attend community events and engage in various conversations, barriers began to break down, and I was increasingly welcomed into different groups. Like experiences of ethnography discussed by Van Maanen, my relationship went from "moving through strangers" with discomfort, isolation, and embarrassment to increased confidence, ease, and comfort (Van Maanen 1988: 2).

I signed up for membership to all three London groups and attended each of their monthly meetings at the Intrepid Fox, Bloomsbury (LVG); the Blue Posts, Piccadilly (VC); and the Devonshire Arms, Camden (LVMG) so that I might observe the naturally occurring activities of the subculture. Alongside the monthly meetings, I also attended various other events in order to get a more informed view of the day-to-day activities offered. These ranged from large-scale events, such as the Halloween disco and the Vampyre Villains versus Steampunk Slayers Costume Showdown Party to smaller, more personal outings, such as fang-fitting parties and visiting participants' homes. As I became more accepted by members of the community, my original concerns over my outsider status began, ironically, to assist my research, as my clothes became a kind of announcement of my researcher status. For example, as my knowledge of the community grew, I began to dress up in period costume for specific events, such as the Halloween and Christmas parties, but maintained a sense of separation by consciously dressing in white and creams as opposed to the communities' favored blacks. This made it easier for members of the community to self-select and become part of my research because I did not necessarily have to make contact with all members of the community for them to know that research was being conducted.

Such trust issues were also appeased by my online exchanges with the community. By using social networking sites, such as Facebook, MySpace, Etsy, Flickr, and LiveJournal as well as more specific vampire sites, such as VEIN (Vampire Exchange Information Network) and the London Vampyre Group forum, I found that I could establish more of a direct contact with members of the group, and issues such as dress were less significant. However, the vast amount of photography available on social networks meant that this issue did not completely dissolve. It is interesting that Hodkinson (2002) had the opposite experience when he conducted online research of the goth community, because he felt that his insider status transformed to that of an outsider online. Hodkinson used photography to reveal his alternative appearance in order to penetrate online community cliques, a problem he had not experienced in face-to-face contexts.

> The most obvious badge of subcultural status—one's physical appearance— becomes devoid when one is communicating with a group of strangers communicating only by e-mail. Therefore, in such forums, the purple and pink streaks in my hair, my piercing, make-up and subculturally distinctive clothing, which have been so useful to most of my research became redundant. In such a situation one must establish subcultural capital—or insider status—only through what one writes. (Hodkinson, personal e-mail, in Mann and Stewart 2000: 90)

In my own experience, as only a partial insider to the subculture, the Internet facilitated my access to the community. It allowed me to reveal aspects of myself that were sympathetic to the subculture, for example, my own interest and knowledge of the subject matter (vampire/horror), and the fashioning of similar gothic aesthetics on my profile page.[10] It also allowed me to communicate my genuine, nonthreatening academic interest in the group. Members of the group began to feel more at ease as they saw other members messages appear on my MySpace and Facebook wall posts. I could also use the network to follow up on face-to-face introductions at meetings, to consolidate contact and aid recruitment.

After one year of frequently attending events and conducting participant observation online, I then began to recruit participants through a process of self-selection. Initially, this begun by posting advertisements for my research on the society websites as well as on my own MySpace, Facebook, and Live-Journal pages, which linked to the community pages on these networks. By this stage I was also directly linked to many of the members on Facebook and MySpace, in particular, as they were added to my friends list over time. Again, social networks were an ideal place to reveal my transparency as a researcher because on profile pages I could clearly state my position as a researcher. I could also provide participants with detailed information regarding the motivations of my study, which assisted with the ethical considerations of achieving informed consent and essentially allowed me to gain trust. It is worth noting that I did not manage to achieve trust in all cases. There were times during the interview process that respondents revealed uneasiness about my motives. For example, during a discussion of the bite fantasy and the pleasures associated with the vampire bite, one respondent revealed her suspicion that my research was concerned with the more sensational, gratuitous depictions of vampire fans:

> Lou: I would never say I sat there and said yes, I would like to get bitten and live forever; it would be great if someone was sat here and said, yeah, I really want to be bitten and then Maria is sat there thinking, "yay result." (Group Interview 1)

VAMPIRE MEMBERS: PARTICIPANT CASE STUDIES

The next chapter will draw upon previous research into subcultures and fan communities, including studies of the goth scene and vampire fans, in order to identify how previous work may be useful to this investigation of vampire culture. The chapter will survey the gendered pleasures that arise during the performance of these vampire femininities and will consider how the externalization of vampire lifestyle can translate to subcultural capital with potential to transform member's status. Before embarking on a discussion of how previous studies into subcultures and fan communities can be updated and reframed, there are some final introductions I would like to make.

While I have achieved data from a wide cross section of the vampire community, throughout this book I have chosen to refer to eight representative case study responses in particular; these are fully documented in Table 1. These case studies have been carefully selected so that they reflect the wider community, as they have varying degrees of vampire dress, online activity, and subcultural status. My motivations behind presenting this research in this manner is to allow the reader the opportunity to get firmly acquainted with these members of the vampire community, so that they may follow their stories, not as examples or as quotes on a page, but as people.

These women include Nancy, the 32-year-old, white/German, published author of vampire novel *Take a Bite*, who is editor of the LVG fanzine *Chronicles*; MorbidFrog, the white/French, 34-year-old university librarian who holds a master's degree and specializes in occult literature, and who is also the new members representative and social secretary for the VC; Jenny, the white/ British, 64-year-old retired grandmother, who has just stepped down from her position of VC organizer and has left the community and moved to Wales with her husband (and vampyre master), Colin; Ronita, the 28-year-old, mixed-race publishing manager who lives in Manchester and commutes to London for vampire-community events; Rebecca, the white/British, 38-year-old city

Table 1 Table of Participants

Case	Membership	Profile
Audrey	VC, LVG, LVMG	Age: 28 Nationality: White/French Marital status: Single Level of dress: Everyday participation (steampunk and vampire) Profession: Creates and sells handcrafted vampire, baroque, and steampunk commodities in her online shop, Enlyl's Realm Social media activity: Active, but uses online resources primarily for professional purposes to sell her handmade items
Nancy	LVG, occasional VC (*Chronicles* vampire fanzine editor)	Age: 32 Nationality: White/German Marital status: In a relationship Level of dress: All events Profession: Education (administrative) and published author Social media activity: Moderate—Facebook
Lou	LVG	Age: 33 Nationality: White/British Marital status: Single Level of dress: Only dresses in vampire style for some events Profession: Marketing Social media activity: Does not use social media
MorbidFrog	VC (new members rep and social secretary), occasional LVG & LVMG	Age: 34 Nationality: White/French Marital status: Single Level of dress: Everyday participation Profession: Librarian (specializes in occult literature) Social media activity: Highly active—LiveJournal, Facebook, MySpace
Rebecca	LVG	Age: 38 Nationality: White/British Marital status: Married Level of dress: Frequent but not daily or for all events Profession: IT program management Social media activity: Often—MySpace, Facebook, LiveJournal
Jenny	VC (previous organizer)	Age: 64 Nationality: White/British Marital status: Married Level of dress: Every day Profession: Retired (administrative) Social media activity: Moderate—LiveJournal, Facebook, MySpace

(Continued)

Table 1 Table of Participants (*Continued*)

Case	Membership	Profile
Ronita (anonymity requested and maintained)	LVMG, VC	Age: 28 Nationality: Mixed race/British Marital status: Single Level of dress: Considers herself alternative and dresses in an alternative manner every day Profession: Publishing manager Social media activity: Frequent—LiveJournal, Facebook, MySpace
Beth (anonymity requested and maintained)	LVG	Age: 30 Nationality: White/British Marital status: Single Level of dress: For events and, where possible, every day Profession: Clerical Social media activity: Moderate—LiveJournal, MySpace

Note: Age, profession, and marital details are documented as they were at the time of this research. VC = Vampyre Connexion; LVG = London Vampyre Group; LVMG = London Vampire Meetup Group.

worker and social secretary for the LVG; Beth, the white/British, 30-year-old pagan office worker; Lou, the 33-year-old, white/British Christian marketing executive; and Audrey, the 28-year-old, white/French jewelry maker and alternative model. The following pages will now tell these women's stories and present a snapshot of vampire culture.

-3-

Vampire Femininity and Status

It is another freezing and drizzly afternoon in London, as the London Vampyre Group assembles in the Argyll Arms, off Oxford Street, for their Victorian pub crawl. Despite the weather, curiosity has gotten the better of me, and I have decided to follow the Victorian theme of the day and dress up a little more than usual, purchasing a white, red, and green corset; cream crinoline; and long, ivory, crinkle cotton overskirt. I have been observing the community for a few years now and feel more comfortable with my selection of clothes because I know that these choices are in keeping with members' styles (although the pale color may not be), and on occasion, Lou, Nancy, and other members of the community have urged me to experiment with my outfit, so I decided that today was the day.

As well as my own curiosity, my choice to dress was motivated by the public nature of the event and the opportunity to take part in a group spectacle. Unlike other vampire meetings that were held in private rooms, the pub crawl involved visiting places that were not typical vampire haunts. I was aware that part of the appeal of this type of public display was tied to presenting a group front, with everyone dressing in their best vampire finery. For instance, previously, comments had been made about the Brighton day trip, and how impressive it was to see twenty vampires all dressed in black, as they emerged over Brighton Pier. Similarly, en route to the London Vampyre Group's excursion to Horace Walpole's Gothic Castle in Strawberry Hill, members expressed their pleasure in being able to partake in normal, everyday activities, such as taking the bus and popping into the shops with friends who were all dressed in vampire clothing.

Therefore, in an effort to avoid being entirely conspicuous, I adhered to the group aesthetic and actually felt like a film star for the day. I suddenly had the opportunity to experiment with theatrical makeup and long, false eyelashes and to wear clothes that I had never worn before: elegant skirts that trailed the floor and a corset that squeezed me into a shape that I never knew I had. It was as though the confines I usually placed upon my wardrobe (in line with what I deemed suitable for a twenty-something lecturer) were suddenly extended, and I had the freedom to play and experiment.

To start the afternoon, we gathered in one of the Argyll Arms' snugs, and Nancy explained the itinerary. This was a pub crawl with a difference; each establishment had been carefully selected for its Victorian architecture, and a short history would be provided at every venue along the way. We visited five pubs in total, including the Argyll Arms, The Tottenham, The Salisbury, The Princess Louise, and The Cittie of Yorke and, overall, the day was a success. There were moments when we stumbled upon some truly gothic parts of London. Wandering around cobbled streets in floor-length bustled skirts, top hats, frock coats, lace parasols, and gold-embellished wooden walking canes provided moments that haunted the past but with a distinctly morbid twist, because although outfits reimagined the historical and particularly Victorian/Edwardian periods, garments were predominantly black and fused with vampire iconography, from silver crucifix jewelry to fangs. This was a historical reimagining of London, but it was a distinctly Bram Stoker, or Robert Louis Stevenson, inspired vision.

As one might expect from such a visible event, the attention that was drawn to the community was not always positive. While I was waiting to be served at the grand mahogany bar in The Salisbury, Covent Garden, I overheard a conversation between two men concerning one of the vampire members. The men were finding it difficult to avert their eyes from her rather generous cleavage, but they were making disparaging remarks about her, due to what they considered to be highly inappropriate, provocative clothing, remarking that "no one wants to see that." The woman in question was wearing a black satin, steel-boned sweetheart corset and, like many women within the community, she was curvaceous and shapely, with an hourglass figure. She used the corset to cinch her waist and support her ample breasts; her skirt was full and covered her legs entirely; it was padded around the hips, which once again drew attention to her reduced waistline and figure-of-eight silhouette.

The woman fashioned a style that I had seen other community member's wear a number of times before, yet the image that she (and wider vampire members) preferred, and may even find beautiful, was clearly at odds with what the men perceived as normal femininity. As Dunja Brill asserts when observing the relationships between gothic women and conventional men, during her account of *Goth Culture: Gender, Sexuality and Style*, these clashes are not uncommon and can be partly attributed to the perceivably hostile image of goth women. Although goth/vampire women may capture the male gaze (it is worth noting that while the men made their remarks, their gaze was not averted for even a moment), wearing dark clothes that convey a sense of morbid fascination, or what Brill refers to as *"femme fatale* overtones," creates a sense of distance that "rattles" men, and prevents their advances, as goth women appear "powerful" and "scary" (Brill 2008: 63).

The incident started me thinking on a number of levels that will form the focus of this chapter. First, it once again underlined the clear tensions and frictions that run between conventional and alternative group and that the vampire community is a place for insiders and outsiders. When witnessing such an unpleasant clash first hand, my own flirtation with wearing vampire clothes suddenly seemed less appealing, as I realized that engaging in experimentation and play came at a price. On the one hand, these items are alternative and do privilege a different look or beauty aesthetic, and with that comes a certain amount of resistance and rejection of the mainstream, but on the other hand, despite empowering potentials, women are not simply left alone to dress and behave how they choose; they are still subject to the same judgments and structuring forces within society that existed before they joined the vampire community. Therefore, this chapter brings together previous literature on gender, subcultures, and fan studies to shed light on precisely what vampire femininity offers to women. Drawing on theories of identity performance, the discussion addresses the subversive potentials of vampire dress and how far these vampire identities can be considered truly empowering, or freeing.

Second, as well as considering the relations between the vampire community and outsiders, the incident also made me contemplate the *internal* social politics within the community, which was comparatively more subtle and less easy to define when compared to the community's relationship with the wider public.[1] Just as the vampire community is not a safe haven that protects members from tensions and antagonisms in the outside world, internally it cannot exist as a utopia, with all members getting along and being organized in exactly the same way. Like any community that is made up of individuals with their own tastes and preferences, the vampire community must be subject to internal fragments, cliques, and hierarchies. I wondered, as I watched the sea of black outfits, what cracks may be forming. Therefore, using Sarah Thornton's theory of subcultural capital, this chapter will also address questions of internal community politics and the measures of vampire community status.

PERFORMING GENDER

When addressing the question of vampire identity and its potential to provide women with a form of empowerment and agency, Judith Butler's work on identity performance is a good place to start. In *Gender Trouble* (1990), Butler asserts that gender identity is an illusion that we retroactively create by performance. Our bodies may be marked by a sex, either male or female, but femininity is culturally inscribed and socially sanctioned. In order to be "girled," we perform a laborious repetition of acts from birth; we are given pink clothes, our hair is grown, and we play with different toys and watch different television programs.

When thinking about Butler's work in relation to the vampire community, it is clear that women are presenting different identities to more normalized, socially sanctioned forms of femininity as they engage with an alternative vampire lifestyle and perform vampire femininities. These alternative vampire performances, like the goths and punks before them, raise questions about the subversive potentials of identity construction and whether they can be viewed as empowering, or freeing. Since *Gender Trouble* was published, two decades have passed and extremely varied interpretations of the original text have arisen, concerning the question of how much control and choice individuals have over their own identity performance.

These disparate viewpoints and reactions to Butler's work are certainly worthy of further consideration because, depending on your position within the debate, identity performance can be seen to offer the subject either entirely *unconstrained* or *constrained* agency. Put another way, women's performance of vampire identity can be interpreted either as being entirely voluntary and subversive or as reactionary—a dichotomy that has already been pointed out by Brill in her study of the goth community (2008: 181). For instance, a reading of the vampire community from the first of these perspectives would suggest that women's performance of vampire identity is subversive because they can select alternative vampire identities in place of socially sanctioned forms of gender and thus experience femininity on their own terms. Alternatively, a reading from the opposing viewpoint would indicate that vampire identities offer limited agency because there are wider structures and forces that maintain gender lines, and those who fall outside these have not achieved power at all, but are positioned as Other.

In order to explore these polarized viewpoints in more detail, and to help us address the question of what vampire femininity may offer to women, we will turn to recent critiques of Butler's work. In her chapter, "No Woman, No Cry?," Angela McRobbie (2005) addresses the limitations of studies that approach Butler's text from celebratory viewpoints. McRobbie suggests that the main misconception of *Gender Trouble* is that it suggests a type of voluntarism and *unconstrained* agency. McRobbie suggests that it could imply that "if gender is an enactment, a crafting on or stylisation of the body according to certain conventions, then gender is also a kind of choice, so that social transformation of gender relations would rest on a simple act of re-designation" (2005: 83). McRobbie makes reference to Campbell and Harbord as she discusses that the note of optimism at the end of *Gender Trouble* may have led to some of these misunderstandings. Campbell and Harbord suggest that there is a sense that "if we don't like or want to be one identity we can perform and act another" (Campbell and Harbord 1999, in McRobbie 2005: 84).

From a poststructuralist point of view, Pierre Bourdieu also identifies the limitations of such celebratory work that fails to take into account that identity is not merely voluntaristic but is predetermined by historical structures. During the preface to *Masculine Domination* (2001), Bourdieu points out that there are various predetermined systems or structures—including interconnected institutions such as the family, the church, the state, the education system, sport, and journalism—that continue to uphold the divide between men and women. He warns that research into the parodic performances of the heroic breaks from conventional routine may produce meager results, without a consideration of the wider social and cultural forces at work:

> One has to ask what are the *historical* mechanisms responsible for the *relative dehistoricization* and *eternalization* of the structure of the sexual division. . . . Combating these historical forces of dehistoricization must be the most immediate objective of an enterprise of mobilization. . . . This strictly *political* mobilization, which would open for women the possibility of a collective action of resistance, orientated towards legal and political reforms, contrast both with the resignation that is encouraged by all essentialist (biological or psychoanalytical) visions of the difference between the sexes and with a resistance that is reduced to individual acts or the endlessly recommended discursive "happenings" that are recommended by some feminist theoreticians—these heroic breaks in the everyday routine, such as the "parodic performances" favoured by Judith Butler, probably expect too much for the meagre and uncertain results they obtain. (Bourdieu 2001: viii)

In *Bodies that Matter* (1993), Butler reveals her own frustrations concerning what she considers a misreading and simplification of her work, and she suggests that such a reading creates a caricature of identity. This misinterpretation proposes that we can go to our wardrobe in the morning, select some clothing, and become free, and then shed these subversive identities at night. She advises researchers to draw on her theory of performativity with caution because researchers must be wary of romanticizing the nature of these subversive identity performances and celebrating these "queer" identities as though they have achieved acts of agency and freedom outside the gender system. Butler closes down the subversive potentials of these performances even further when she suggests that any association made to active agents who can cause gender trouble, and change or overturn assumptions about gender, would be to completely ignore the success of the power system and the structures that maintain the heterosexual matrix:

> Matters have been made worse, if not more remote, by the questions raised by the notion of gender performativity introduced in *Gender Trouble*. For if I were to argue that genders are performative, that could mean that I thought that one woke in the morning, perused the closet or some more open space for the gender of choice, donned that gender for the day, and then restored the garment to its place at night. Such a willful and instrumental subject, one who decides on its gender, is clearly not its gender from the start and fails to realize that its existence is already decided *by* gender. (Butler 1993: x)

Therefore, viewing the performance of vampire femininity from a celebratory platform as an entirely voluntaristic act is certainly problematic because it does not acknowledge the wider structures and forces that impact on women's everyday lives. However, approaching these vampire performances from the reverse perspective—as being entirely *constrained* or devoid of agency—is equally not without issue because such readings leave no room for independent choice and render the performer entirely powerless to the hegemonic power of the heterosexual matrix. As Dunja Brill points out in her study of goth culture, although Butler's work on "drag" doesn't completely rule out the idea that individuals may be able to actively subvert the gender system, Butler's approach really does close down the possibilities by which agency can be achieved:

> [Butler's] notion of the hegemonic power of the heterosexual matrix and its binary gender discourse is problematic, however, as it poses this discourse as seemingly all-encompassing and monolithic. Although Butler's position does not completely exclude the possibility of subversive acts within the gender system, the agency of the subject to challenge the dominant discourse is bounded by strict limits. (Brill 2008: 18)

We therefore find ourselves in difficult territory when thinking about just what these alternative vampire performances offer to women, falling somewhere between two camps. Although we cannot entirely rid women of any acts of agency in these performances— because, at the very least, fashioning the vampire draws attention to the naturalization of gender ideals within society and, indeed, some women have expressed conscious ideologies of power and agency throughout this research—it is equally important to avoid producing celebratory accounts of the vampire community. If throughout this book I was to argue that through their subversive identity performances the vampire community had achieved some "form of visionary cultural revolution" (Brill 2008: 34) and had successively challenged the traditional constructs of femininity, gaining real freedom outside of the heterosexual matrix, then this research would have failed to note the complexity of the gender systems that hold them in place. For example, such a reading would ignore the level of negotiation that is occurring within these identity performances and how many women may choose to conceal, or may be forced to conceal, their identities in wider contexts (such as work). Similarly, as the example of the disparaging remarks made about the vampire member on the Victorian pub crawl suggests, such a reading would also fail to recognize the Othering of the community by wider society and the consequent sniggers, rudeness, and abuse that is continually dealt to members. As McRobbie asserts, any such reading of Butler's work would undermine those who routinely remain outside of the sanctioned gender system, who are constantly dealt pain and injuries (2005: 87).

But with the greatest significance, which will be dealt with in detail later in this chapter, a reading of Butler's work that viewed vampire femininities from an entirely celebratory perspective would also ignore the fact that these identities still maintain and reinforce traditional gender lines. Although vampire identity may draw attention to the constructed nature of identity on the whole, women continue to reproduce heterosexual gender roles, as vampire outfits reimagine a historical, and particularly a *feminine*, gender identity. Therefore, vampire femininities do not overthrow the gender system. In fact, they do the opposite, as women's identity performances actually maintain as opposed to threaten or wreak havoc with traditional ideas about gender.

Therefore, as this section has already established, we cannot view these vampire performances as being entirely empty of subversive or challenging ideas because this book is concerned with discovering precisely why women elect to fashion vampire lifestyles and what these vampire identities offer them; but, equally, we must not approach the vampire subculture from an uncritical, celebratory perspective, viewing it as an entirely resistive microcosm of idyllic community life, free from—and entirely separate from—the so-called mainstream. And why would we want to? It is precisely the ways in which the vampire community negotiate their alternative interests on a daily basis, amid their lives in the real world—around work, friends, and families—that is the really interesting issue here, and one that will be the main subject of this study.

The specific (micro)structures, hierarchies, frictions, antagonisms, and contradictory experiences that flow directly through, as opposed to along-side, the vampire community provide much more titillating lines of enquiry, as opposed to viewing the community as an entirely resistive subculture, free from the pressures of the outside world. Issues of status, how one can be rich or poor in subcultural knowledge, how well known high-profile members arise, are all at the center of this research. Drawing on previous studies of subcultures, the following section will now move on to address the second focus of this chapter, which is concerned with issues of internal community politics and status.

SUBCULTURAL CAPITAL: BEING "IN THE KNOW"

Since the early 1920s, a great deal of research has been conducted into sub-cultural theory. During the 1940s and 1950s, academics working within the Chicago School of Sociology (see Cressey 1932; Gordon 1947; A. K. Cohen 1955/1997) focused on urban sociology, street culture, and "the extraordinary diversity of human behaviour in the American city" (Gelder and Thornton 1997: 3). As Hodkinson asserts, although the emphasis of individual theorists varied, the school is perhaps better known for its "conception of subcultures as deviant groups" (2002: 9). During the 1970s, researchers such as Dick Hebdige, who was working at the Centre of Contemporary Cultural Studies (CCCS) in Birmingham University, went on to investigate spectacular youth subcultures and the meaning of style.

The Birmingham School analyzed how cultural objects were borrowed and reappropriated by mainly working-class groups, such as punks and skinheads, as a form of social resistance and rebellion. For instance, in *Subculture: The Meaning of Style* (1979), Hebdige uses the example of the punk and how members of this group select objects in a deliberate attempt to subvert their original connotations and meanings for anarchy because they set out to use style to disrupt meaning in the form of Vivienne Westwood's "confrontation dressing": "A pin, a plastic clothes peg, a television component, a razor blade, a tampon—could be brought within the province of punk (un) fashion" (1979: 107). During his section on homology, Hebdige identifies a paradox at the heart of subcultural style, in that the nonconformist, resistive styles often associated with youth sub-cultures are actually thoroughly ordered and consistent or, to borrow a term from Lévi-Strauss, "homologous" (1979: 113). Hebdige states that the punk subculture had "a homological relation between the trashy cut-up clothes and spiky hair, the pogo and amphetamines, the spitting, the vomiting, the format of the fanzines" (1979: 114), which underlines the inherent pleasure of belonging and conforming to a group, albeit an alternative group.

Hebdige's ideas of adhering to a group aesthetic resonate with the vampire community, that places a certain amount of emphasis on group spectacle and public display, but this type of approach to spectacular subcultures has its limitations, and the work of Stanley Cohen and, particularly, Sarah Thornton are more useful to draw upon for this study. For instance, Cohen (1972, 2002) and Thornton (1995) critiqued the work of the Birmingham School and have highlighted the limitations of approaching subcultures from this "spectacular" vantage point, suggesting that a general "demystification" of subcultures must be achieved, and future research must place less emphasis on decoding subcultural objects, and more emphasis on the ordinariness of members' everyday lives (Gelder and Thornton 1997: 146).

For instance, in his discussion of "Symbols of Trouble" in *Folk Devils and Moral Panics*, Stanley Cohen asserts that instead of attempting to see subcultures as entirely resistive and anchored in class issues, researchers must focus on how members of such groups experience the more mundane aspects of ordinary, everyday life. Cohen states that future research on the more ordinary aspects of subcultural lifestyle is needed to "give a sense of the concrete—some feeling of time and space; when and how the styles and symbols fit into the daily round of the home, work or school, friendship" (2002: lxii). While Hebdige's work is useful because it highlights that the meaning of subcultural style may be about belonging and conforming, each subculture may not always be homologous but, in contrast, may experience internal hierarchies, cliques, and variations on what marks out the boundaries of the group.

In "The Social Logic of Subcultural Capital" (1997), Thornton uses the example of club cultures to outline the various ways that people engage in subcultural lifestyle and the internal power relations and microstructures that form within each group. Drawing on the work of Bourdieu and his ideas of cultural capital set out in *Distinction: A Social Critique of the Judgement of Taste* (1984), Thornton coins the phrase "subcultural capital." She uses the theory to demonstrate that not all members of a subculture experience group lifestyle in the same way but instead take up a number of different positions that are dependent on the amount of subcultural capital they possess. Thornton identifies that one of the main advantages of Bourdieu's work is that he approaches social structure as a highly complex and fragmentary space, with factors of cultural, economic, and social capital, and further subcategories of *linguistic*, *academic*, *intellectual*, *information*, and *artistic* capital. Thornton explains subcultural capital in relation to cultural capital:

> Subcultural capital confers status on its owner in the eyes of the relevant be-holder. It affects the standing of the young in many ways like its adult equiva-lent. Subcultural capital can be objectified and embodied. Just as books and paintings display cultural capital in the family home, so subcultural capital is objectified in the form of fashionable haircuts and carefully assembled record collections. . . . Just as cultural capital is personified in "good" manners and urbane conversation, so subcultural capital is embodied in the form of being "in the know." (1995: 11)

The theory of subcultural capital, and Thornton's concept of hipness, is very useful to this study. Although Thornton's work is focusing principally on youth subcultures, it is important to acknowledge that there has been an ex-tension of youth, and members of the vampire community are actively engag-ing in community interests up until the age of sixty-five (for instance, Jenny is a Vampyre Connexion member and a grandmother). Therefore, Thornton's work is to be thought of less in terms of age and more in terms of how people acquire subcultural capital—how they become in the know and hip. On re-flection, the speed in which subcultural capital transforms as things go from being cutting edge and popular to old hat and antiquated is forever escalat-ing. Even the word *hip* is now an outdated term. Therefore, trying to ascertain how one becomes cool, trendy, and popular at any given point in a transient subculture is no easy feat, as interests, clothes, fiction, and clubs quickly go in and out of fashion. One way to channel these conflicting and ever-changing taste patterns is to harness the media that circulates within the community.

SUBCULTURAL MEDIA

As Thornton asserts during her discussion of Bourdieu's theory of cultural capital, one of the major differences between her own work and that of Bourdieu's is the value that she places on subcultural media. Print media such as newspapers, journals, magazines, flyers and online social media such as Facebook, LiveJournal, and MySpace as well as community-specific websites and networks play an absolutely vital role in the consolidation and regulation of community life. One's position in the group, of being in or out, high or low in subcultural capital, is contingent on one's consumption and, increasingly, production of subcultural media.

Publications that circulate the vampire community, such as *Dark Nights* and *Chronicles* fanzines, both document and inform community politics and lifestyle. From just a quick flick through the endless back issues of community fanzines that I have accumulated over the period of this research, it is possible to identify important information about vampire community lifestyle, which can transform the reader to being "in the know." For instance, fanzines contain reviews of popular vampire fictions, such as *Dracula: Pages from a Virgin's Diary*, *I Am Legend*, *30 Days of Night*, and *True Blood*, as well as those that are not so popular, such as the BBC's 2006 version of *Dracula*. The publications also include vampire fashion features, articles on recent events, such as the London Vampyre Group's trip to Prague, and tongue-in-cheek articles on subcultural lifestyle. For instance, the *Chronicles* includes a feature titled "Methods of Goth Dance: Polishing your Technique," with illustrated goth dance moves, such as The Matador, Drying the Fingernails, Pagan Pushbike, and Uppercut the Dwarf, and articles that highlight the hazards of vampire dress, which include topics such as getting pointy feet from wearing pointy boots and having to hairspray your face to keep your makeup in place.

As well as collating subcultural information that can make the reader in the know, these publications reflect the frictions and contradictions that separate members of the community and prevent them from being a cohesive or entirely homogenous grouping. For instance, the *Chronicles* "Letters" section documents examples of conflicting attitudes and community politics. Lou is a practicing Christian and a member of the London Vampyre Group. She recently wrote a letter to the editor of *Chronicles* fanzine, in response to the positive review of Richard Dawkins's book *The God Delusion*, which was included in the previous month's issue. In her letter, Lou states that she is a "vampire loving, metal-listening, eye-liner abusing Goth . . . who is proud to be a card carrying member of the LVG as well as the God Squad" (Schumann 2007). She defends her belief in Christianity, which may run counter to other members of the community's views, but asserts that this does not make her delusional or mentally weak.

Similarly, the "Letters" section also includes a complaint from a reader concerning an article that was published about blood drinking. The article in question included in-depth information on sanguinarian groups and an interview with Johann, a blood fetishist. The complaint, made by vampire community member North Wind, voices concerns about whether the article fits in with the wider London Vampyre Group ethos, as the community has recently taken steps to educate those outside of the community that it is not a blood cultist society. The complaint states that "I thought that the revamped website always made a point of not promoting blood drinking or fetishism, and yet you have a long article about just that in your last issue" (Schumann 2006). Nancy, the editor of *Chronicles*, responds to the complaint in partial agreement. She acknowledges that the article was in fact debated among the editorial team and states that she anticipated a controversial response from readers. However, Nancy explains that the article presented the team with an ideal opportunity to cover a challenging and sensitive topic and to "show just what we are not about" (Schumann 2006). The exchange between North Wind and Nancy demonstrates that the community may be united on the wider issue of blood cultism—in that the vampire community excludes blood-drinking activities—but it also highlights that the way in which such issues are approached and handled on a daily basis is up for debate and often meet controversy and disagreement.

Subcultural media also reveal another important aspect of subcultural life that is tied up with the economies, or more aptly, the microeconomies of the subculture. Thornton applies Bourdieu's principles of economic capital to her own definition of subcultural capital and states that while subcultural capital may not be as profitable and financially viable as cultural capital, a range of subcultural businesses do emerge, from night-club organizers to record industry professionals. Thornton goes on to suggest that community members, who take up professions linked to the subculture, can increase their "respect" and status within the community. She states that in some cases, these members may even define the very currencies of subcultural capital within the community (1995: 203).

These issues of microeconomies are also of interest to this study. Since the proliferation of social media sites, the potential for subcultural income revenues has expanded as online profiles document a range of activities, including member's alternative photo shoots, vampire fan artwork, jewelry making, and vampire/horror film special effects work. Social media has also facilitated members' accumulation of subcultural capital— in some cases, members can champion the technology and afford themselves high-profile status. For instance, MorbidFrog, the social secretary for the Vampyre Connexion, is a particularly well-known member of the community. MorbidFrog was an early adopter of new social technologies, and members have come to rely heavily upon the information she imparts. Such high-profile members of the community are important to consider in detail (see chapter 6), but it is also crucial to refrain from merely interviewing these celebrity members. Therefore, this book will also account for how other members of the community use social media for creative and economic motivations. For instance, Audrey uses her Facebook and Etsy profiles to market and sell her baroque jewelry and to promote herself as an alternative model; Jenny uses Facebook and MySpace to exhibit her gothic-themed artwork; and Nancy, who has recently published her own nonfiction book, *Take a Bite*, which explores female vampires in folklore, uses her Facebook profile to announce book launches and to link her potential readership to the Amazon website for payment methods. Conversely, Lou refuses to sign up to a social media account, and the consequences of not having a social media profile will also be considered.

As this section demonstrates, subcultural capital is clearly an extremely useful concept to explore throughout this book, as it provides opportunities to investigate precisely what constitutes subcultural capital in the vampire community and how members are organized across hierarchies, cliques, and fragments (this is explored in detail throughout chapter 6). However, although it is a useful theory, there are some drawbacks to Thornton's approach that this study seeks to address. As Brill (2008) quite rightly notes, despite the strengths of Thornton's work, she has not accounted for the specifically gendered currencies of subcultural capital. Brill states that

> Thornton (1995) fails to consider gendered economies of capital which might take different forms for males and females, despite citing some observations pointing in that direction. For instance, she mentions clothes—which have traditionally been more closely linked to female status attainment—an important part of subcultural capital; she names "the size of a *man's* record collection" (Ibid., p. 118, original emphasis) as a classic measure of it; she quotes an author positing clubs as "classless" spaces where success is the mains status criterion and, for girls, physical beauty (Ibid., p. 55). But nowhere does she follow up these hints to propose potentially *different* spheres of measures for male and female subcultural distinction. (2008: 35)

Therefore, as the next section will explore in detail, my analysis of the vampire community is not only concerned with subcultural capital and with establishing how members achieve privileged positions within the vampire community, and equally, how they may not; but also with investigating the specifically *feminine* patterns of vampire community lifestyle and how these female spheres of measures may translate to subcultural capital.

BEING ONE OF THE GIRLS

Turning to studies of fan cultures for a moment, Joanne Hollows's work also illustrates the need for updated research into the specifically *feminine* pursuits of subcultural capital. In "The Masculinity of Cult" (2003), Hollows discusses the gendering of traditional, pre-Internet and DVD cult consumption as masculine, examining the use of the "sleazo" movie theater and the emergence of the Midnight Movie. She notes that fan cults are often viewed as a subculture and thus by regarding them this way we must concede that the concept of subcultures are naturalized as male. She draws on Thornton (1995) as she argues that "mainstream cinema is imagined as feminized mass culture and cult as a heroic and masculinized subculture" (2003: 37). Hollows points out that this is not to imply that female fans were denied the privilege of watching cult movies and the pleasure of reading and responding to them in feminine ways, but rather that they may have adopted masculine consumption patterns of viewing (i.e., where they watched, and how they accessed the films), which relocated their position to "culturally one of the boys" (Thornton 1995, in Hollows 2003: 35).[2]

In opposition to these findings, cult films have recently been made much more accessible, altering viewing habits, and thus the barriers for women watching these texts have dissolved. More women can now freely admit to being fans, and, consequently, female fans have gained a higher profile; thus, more female patterns of cult fandom have emerged. Women can watch shows in their homes on television, DVD, and the Internet, as opposed to the "sleazo" movie theater. This is not to suggest that Hollows's work is erroneous because she has consciously framed her discussion historically. It does, however, reveal the need to update the research in this area of female cult fans and their position in fan culture because significant developments have taken place.

Just as the introduction of new technologies such as the video and DVD formats from the 1980s and 1990s allowed women to engage with cult films and television in more feminized ways (as opposed to the Midnight Movie circuit), the development of social media technologies has also had a notable impact on feminine fan pursuits. As a result of the widespread use of social media sites, women are feeling more confident and therefore more able to practice their fandom. Social networks are opening up feminine fan practices, as they offer women a place to act out their interests and also allow women to seek out other women who participate in these practices.

Social media sites have been integral to the development of wider fan communities, such as female fans of horror media, because women can contribute to horror discussions, post their own horror films online, keep up to date with information about horror festivals and events, and be part of a community of other women who share similar interests. The article "Women: It's a Scream" (Roby 2008: 14) that appeared in the *Guardian*'s *G2* magazine, investigated the female fascination with horror. The article suggests that innovations in new media technologies, and principally social networking sites, have provided women with a dialogue to experience their fandom in a safe space. The article cites social media sites, such as Ax Wound[3] ("gender in the horror genre") and Pretty-Scary.net[4] as online forums where women can engage in discussions about their horror fandom. As well as online forums, the article suggests that women are increasingly engaging in horror fan activities, such as attending festivals. As Adèle Hartley, the event creator of the Dead by Dawn festival, notes, there has been a change in audience demographic in recent years that has challenged the "boys in black zombie T-shirts" stereotype. "When Hartley started Dead by Dawn 15 years ago, only a handful of women attended. These days the audience is split 50/50" (Roby 2008: 14).

Therefore, a lot has changed since Thornton's research on club cultures and Hollow's historical study of cult film fans. This study is primarily concerned with the female attachment to the vampire and explores whether the vampire subculture offers women the chance to respond to their fandom in particularly feminine ways, such as the more typical female traits of shopping, wearing makeup, and making/wearing clothes, as opposed to being culturally one of the boys.

EXCESSIVE FEMININITY

Alongside these feminine modes of consumption, the identities that women constitute are also inherently feminine, revealing a discourse of excessive femininity within the vampire community. This excessive femininity has been identified in wider fan communities and subcultures. For example, Paul Hodkinson establishes in *Goth* (2002) that gothic style is closely associated with femininity and ambiguity. Hodkinson notes that goths of both genders can wear an array of apparel that is more traditionally associated with the feminine, from jewelry, makeup, and Victorian frilly shirts to skirts and fishnets.[5] He suggests that the goth scene opens up gender distinctions and allows a space for men to not only be proud of more effeminate, slim, hairless bodies but also to engage in more feminine, socially sanctioned behavior, such as displays of emotion and "same sex tactility" (Hodkinson 2002: 54). As Hodkinson points out, while performing such gender ambiguities is much more about fashioning an aesthetic and is distinct from people's sexual preference, there is quite often a feeling of acceptance for bisexual and same-sex relations. Hodkinson considers various reasons for such acceptance but suggests that this can be mainly attributed to the gradual blurring of female and male gender distinctions, which have allowed for new ways of thinking about gender as separate and distinct from sex.

Brill, in her ethnography of the goth community, continues on similar research lines to Hodkinson. She states that unlike the highly masculinized spaces of subcultures (e.g., such as those discussed by Hollows [2003]), the goth subculture is often viewed as a feminine space, as even male participants privilege female aesthetics, selecting long hair and makeup that are traditionally feminine traits. Brill asserts that while men might fashion androgynous styles, the opposite is true for women, as they present hyperfeminine displays, in what Brill terms as the "cult of femininity" for *both* sexes (2008: 41). This cult of femininity is especially linked to achieving subcultural status and means very different things for men and women. According to Brill, when fashioned by male goths, these feminine displays provide "stark opposition to traditional gender stereotypes of style and appearance," but when presented by women, "such a look assumes very different meaning, as it is far more in accord with common cultural norms of femininity" (2008: 42). Therefore, these hyperfeminine displays by goth women serve to reinforce and uphold traditional gender lines; further still (and as this book seeks to uncover), they may even trap women into a particular type of look, as, according to Brill, those women who opt for androgynous appearances in the goth scene (i.e., they wear less makeup and dress in trousers) do not enjoy the same rewards of subcultural capital as androgynous men.

> As Gothic style for both sexes prizes femininity, gender-bending as a source of subcultural capital and status works only for male Goths. What is more, the ideal of hyperfemininity the Gothic subculture espouses for women means that female androgyny is strongly discouraged. Even moderate deviations—like wearing less make-up or short hair—from the excessively feminine image which is the norm for Goth women can cause feelings of somehow being out of place on the scene. (2008: 42)

Going back to my own research of the vampire community, as the outfits worn on the Victorian pub crawl demonstrate, I have also identified excessive femininity within the vampire community that will be explored. The clothes that women wear construct a specifically historical and morbid take on femininity, as by women's own admission, selecting predominantly Victorian/Edwardian identities allows them to reimagine themselves in a time when "women were women." This is in stark contrast to contemporary mainstream fashion, with women often wearing more casual clothing in everyday contexts, such as jeans and T-shirts. I will therefore consider if the cult of femininity extends to all women and whether there are exceptions to this image. I will also document what these excessively feminine displays reveal about women's attitudes and opinions, as throughout this research I have observed that women's outlooks certainly do not reflect the same old-fashioned Victorian values that match their clothes.

In contrast, women have frequently used their excessively feminine vampire identities to articulate strong female ideas, often stating that these clothes made them feel more confident and strong. Milly Williamson's research of the vampire fans in the UK and United States also highlights this tension. Williamson argues that the women from her study expressed a sense of not fitting in to the predominant cultural construction of femininity. She suggests that this sense of isolation has consequently led to women's internalization of an alternative ideal. Such ideals are then performed and exteriorized through an "alternative sartorial identity," as women use dress to demonstrate their defiant sense of "standing out" as different (2001a: 153). Williamson notes how the female vampire fans of her study use dress to reclaim power over traditional constructs of femininity. She states that although these women may be continuing to define themselves in terms of appearance, they are actually selecting alternative, nonconformist but essentially feminine identities (2001a: 149). This idea that the female vampire fans of Williamson's study are simultaneously imagining identities that are more feminine, thus upholding socially sanctioned ideas about gender, and also resistive and nonconformist, brings this research full circle, as we return to the question of the subversive potentials of vampire femininity.

To draw this chapter to a close so that the major findings of this study can be presented, I must attempt to make sense of all these seemingly contradictory points of view. As highlighted during the earlier discussion of Butler's (1990) research, there are clearly two conflicting viewpoints that need to be resolved—that of the subversive and reactionary viewpoints of subcultural lifestyle. If, as discussed previously, these vampire femininities are reinforcing traditional gender lines, then how can they also be used to exert women's real-world strength and power? Are women not taking simultaneous steps forward and back? As Brill points out during her conclusion, if women are using these hyperfeminine identities to articulate agency, then are these performances not entirely undermined by the fact that they draw the attention of the male gaze, and the "to be looked-at-ness" of women (2008: 181)? Also, I cannot presume that all members of the vampire community are fashioning styles for specific, fully thought-out reasons. How many of these women wander around with carefully encoded outfits, just ready for audiences to decode as being teamed with gender subversion and feminine strength? As Cohen suggests, "it would be absurd to demand here that every bearer of symbols walks around with structuralist theory in [her] head" (S. Cohen 1987/1997: 164).

But if these feminine performances are not subversive, then what are they? The situation cannot be so bleak to suggest that vampire dress simply upholds traditional gender lines and transforms women into alternative eye candy. Such a reading does not account for women's potential to use the sartorial vampire to acquire subcultural capital, generate income streams, and raise ones status to that of subcultural celebrity. Therefore, throughout this book I will investigate just what the performance of a pseudohistorical vampire identity offers to women. I will heed advice from McRobbie, Bourdieu, Butler, and Brill and walk the fine line between producing uncritical, celebratory research while also avoiding traps of being too reductive and closing down the subversive potentials of vampire identity entirely.

To assist this investigation of vampire culture, I have extrapolated some of the main issues that have arisen throughout this chapter and have arranged them into four smaller research questions, which are outlined below. The following chapter will sketch a profile of the vampire community and begin to address the first of these questions—who makes up the vampire community, and what does membership involve? Community demographics, lifestyle activities, and creative practices will be presented. The subsequent chapters "Feminine Discourses" and "Alternative Celebrity" will then continue to address these questions and present the major findings of this research.

RESEARCH QUESTIONS

- How is vampire culture fashioned and commodified by members of the community?
- What gendered discourses have emerged from the vampire community, and are there exceptions to the cult-of-femininity rule? How far are women using excessively feminine identities to express strong female attitudes and opinions?
- What equates to subcultural status in the vampire community, and how do you become in the know? What specifically feminine currencies are available?
- What antagonisms, tensions, and contradictory experiences are present within the vampire community?

$-4-$

Vampire Community Profile

The aim of this chapter is to provide a crash course in vampire lifestyle in order to explain *who* members of the vampire community are, *what* types of activities they engage in, as well as accounting for *where* and *when* these (seemingly invisible) vampire community events take place. Unlike the chapters that follow, which are based on qualitative analysis of vampire community interviews and observations, this chapter is presented as an evidential report. It is intended to provide a background profile of the community based on descriptive analysis of the questionnaire data so that deeper issues of gendered discourses, subcultural capital, and community conflicts can be developed later in this book. The following pages will use various media, including photography and charts, to present a rich tapestry of vampire lifestyle, focusing on member's demographics, social life, dress, creativity, and consumption of vampire media.

DEMOGRAPHICS: AGE, BACKGROUND, AND SOCIAL SITUATION

To date, no research has been conducted into the demographics of the female vampire community in London. Therefore, it is now important to establish a profile of the vampire community, taking into consideration respondents' age, nationality, education, occupation, sexuality, and religion so that we can ascertain just *who* are the members of the vampire community[1].

From the questionnaire data, it is evident that the majority of vampire-community respondents are in their late twenties and early thirties (see Figure 2). Although this research captured interview data from women outside of this age bracket, including in-depth data of Jenny, the 64-year-old grandmother,[2] the majority of participants that elected to take part in the in-depth interviews (that will be discussed over the next two chapters) were in their twenties and early thirties.

Because this study was conducted in Britain, the majority of women who took part are British and living in London. However, the sample contains an eclectic range of nationalities, including nationals from France, Germany,

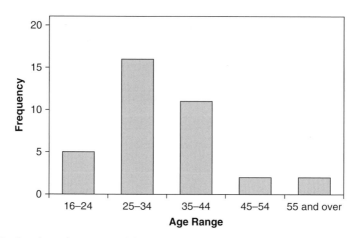

Figure 2   Bar chart of women participants' age

Poland, Holland, New Zealand, Australia, United States, and Mexico. Women are educated, with the majority achieving at least a higher education qualification, and a significant proportion have progressed to study at postgraduate level, either completing master's degrees or, in the case of one participant, a PhD. The percentage of women who left education after completing secondary school is comparatively low (3 percent).

Respondents work in a wide range of occupations. The largest group consists of office and administrative workers. Other occupations include librarianships, the education sector, caring professions, the creative/film industry, management, business, finance, engineering, and IT. Just over half of the women from the sample are married or in a relationship, and relationships are predominantly heterosexual. A small percentage of the women are bisexual (12 percent) and lesbian (3 percent). The most commonly listed religion was Christianity, with the next significant proportion of women belonging to neo-pagan/Wiccan[3] religions.

The relatively high proportion of women who belong to Wiccan religions is not unexpected, given women's interest in the vampire and its potential to draw people who have interests in alternative spirituality and the wider occult. The number of Christian vampire members is more surprising, but on closer inspection, women's shared interest in both vampires and Christianity is not as strange as it may first appear. Vampire members who have been brought up frequenting Christian churches have highlighted similarities between Christian and vampire iconography, and in some cases women have expressed an almost nostalgic familiarity with Christian symbolism, which they now enjoy watching in vampire media. For instance, Christian symbols such as the crucifix, holy water, chalices, and drinking blood (of Christ) are central to vampire mythology. One participant, MorbidFrog, explained how she is now a Wiccan but grew up in a strong Roman Catholic household. During interviews she drew parallels with her own Catholic childhood and vampire film iconography, suggesting that she has always been drawn to these aesthetics and even feels at home with them. She joked that as a child she used to rebel against her Catholic parents by inverting all the crucifixes in the house (inverted crucifixes have been linked to satanic symbolism).

Therefore, through analyzing data collected on respondents' nationality, education, occupation, religion, and sexuality, it is evident that the female vampire community member is in her late twenties/early thirties, predominantly British, middle class, and heterosexual. She is well educated, most probably holding at least an undergraduate degree, and may be either married or single. She may also belong to either Christian or Wiccan religions. Although this research did capture data from non-white community members (including an in-depth interview with Ronita, a mixed-race goth vampire), it emerged from the data collected during participant observations that she is also more likely to be white. So, on reflection, the vampire community is not as diverse and cosmopolitan as its edgy subject matter might at first suggest. In fact, the vampire community seems to have cultural blinkers of its own, as members are predominantly straight, white, and Western.

THE VAMPIRE COMMUNITY AND LIFESTYLE

Having ascertained some basic information concerning the demographics of the vampire community, this section will now outline the specific aspects of vampire-community lifestyle and investigate *what* being part of the vampire community entails. It will account for *where* and *when* specific activities take place, how respondents first encountered the vampire community, and the nature of the fan community and its links with identity subculture.

Activities

The vampire community offers a variety of activities, ranging from obscure events, such as carve your own tombstone, gothic belly dancing, and Kensal Green Cemetery walks to more regular pub and club nights at alternative venues, such as The Dev (the Devonshire Arms, Camden), the Intrepid Fox, Slimelight, and Torture Garden. The most popular events listed by respondents were the alternative Christmas and Halloween parties (89 percent of respondents attended), which are themed costume parties, such as Silent Night: Rest in Pieces Christmas Party, which include music, drinking, and general socializing. The monthly community meetings hosted at private rooms in central London locations, including the Blue Posts, the Intrepid Fox, and the Devonshire Arms also scored highly with respondents (82 percent of respondents attended). These are more regular community events, which provide the opportunity to dress up in vampire fashion, gather around tables, eat, drink, and catch up. They are an important part of the community lifestyle, as they are a dependable date on the vampire calendar. On occasion, vampire book sales, organized talks, and alternative jewelry stands insert offered, but generally, these evenings are reserved for mingling and catching up with friends.

Other popular excursions include Lincoln's "Weekend at the Asylum" Steampunk Festival, one of the larger steampunk events in the UK, which provides the opportunity to fashion one's finest steampunk finery and experience steampunk music, comedy, arts, and crafts. Whitby Goth Weekend, which is a twice-yearly festival held at the fictional setting of Bram Stoker's *Dracula* (which attracts goths both nationally and internationally), and Wave Gotik Treffen Festival in Leipzig, Germany (another large-scale annual goth festival) are also popular. The least popular events were outings to the theater (22 percent attended) and organized quizzes (22 percent attended).

As these events demonstrate, community members are privileging activities such as alternative music and entertainment, dressing in vampire style, and generally meeting up with other members of the community as opposed to activities that are specifically associated with intellectual vampire fan pursuits (e.g., vampire quizzes and literary societies). This suggests that the vampire community places a strong emphasis on socializing, as opposed to being a forum for exchanges about the vampire. So while this should not suggest that members are not consuming vampire fiction (as the final section demonstrates), it does reveal that members would rather spend their time taking part in a subculture, dressing in alternative vampire trends and listening to music genres, such as goth industrial and operatic metal, as opposed to engaging in in-depth discussions about vampire media.

Similarly, data collected from respondents concerning how they first joined the community continue to reflect strong links with subcultural lifestyle and demonstrates an overlap with other alternative communities. For instance, when I asked members their reasons for joining the vampire community, the most popular answer was to "experience something different" (71 percent) followed by the opportunity "to meet new people" (68 percent) and "to dress up" (54 percent). Only half of respondents stated that they joined the group to "talk about vampires" (51 percent). This demonstrates that only half of the community desires to engage in debates about vampires, and that subcultural lifestyle activities such as vampire dress, socializing, and having experiences outside the mainstream are also very important factors.

My own conversations with vampire members at events also revealed that a significant proportion joined the community as a result of their wider immersion into goth lifestyle. They often remarked that they had picked up flyers for the London Vampyre Group, Vampyre Connexion, and London Vampyre Meetup Group at other alternative venues, such the Devonshire Arms and the Intrepid Fox, and then went along to events with friends who were already part of alternative scenes. Others noted that they saw information about vampire events online, on friends' social media sites and then later attended.

Therefore, the vampire community's strong desire to engage in subcultural lifestyle activities is in little doubt. However, the fan nature of the community is somewhat less certain, as women do not appear to be articulating a strong fanatical "love" for their "beloved" vampire texts (Jenkins 1992: 50). In fact, evidence suggests that a small number of community members would not consider themselves to be fans of the vampire at all.

Fans or Subculture?

When asked the question, "Are you a vampire fan?," the majority of women answered *yes* on the questionnaire. However, a small proportion saw vampires simply as an extension of their alternative lifestyle (25 percent), commenting that they were not actually specific fans of the vampire. They wrote statements such as, "No. It is just all part of the Gothic genre and great fun!" (VC30, Questionnaire) and "Not really. I love vampires but this is really a consequence of me being a goth" (LVG28, Questionnaire). One participant also noted how her membership of SLUGS (South London Uber Goths) meant that she was involved in all the goth-related groups in London, including the vampire community.

Therefore, the vampire community seems to be more focused on subcultural interests as opposed to being a traditional vampire fan community. This poses certain challenges for members who join the community with the intention of engaging in more traditional fan pursuits. It appears that women who are fascinated with the vampire and desire to engage in intellectual discussions about vampire fiction and folklore are forced to seek out other communities that better suit their needs. For instance, Jenny has been an extremely active member of the vampire community for approximately fifteen years and has become the figurehead of the Vampyre Connexion; she identifies a shift in the cultural activities of the group—from activities associated with the traditional literary vampire to more social and music nights—that has been partly responsible for her recent decamp from Vampyre Connexion duties. When asked about community events, she commented that "it has become more gig orientated. That is not why we got it into it. We wanted to visit Strawberry Hill House, the Victorian gothic, masked balls, read Wilkie Collins, because Bram Stoker was that period. People are not as keen on that side any more" (Jenny, Questionnaire).

As Jenny asserts, although part of this shift may be due to age and younger members of the group's consequent involvement with activities that are associated with youth cultures (such as dress and music), it also highlights the importance of the more performative aspects of the subculture. Similarly, during my first meeting at the London Vampyre Group, I was introduced to Sarah,[4] who was also attending the community event for the first time. Sarah was not dressed in an alternative manner, although she did wear dark clothes and revealed tattoos that she later told me would usually be covered. During our brief conversation, she mentioned that she had previously attempted to attend a Vampyre Connexion event but had felt extremely awkward when doing so, as the community had not been particularly welcoming or easy to penetrate; in fact, she found it rather alienating for outsiders. Sarah suggested that she wanted to attend vampire events so that she could talk to other women about their interest in vampire literature, as her everyday life as a wife and mother was so far removed from her interests in the gothic. Sarah noted that her experience of the London Vampyre Community was also not what she had expected, commenting that the loud music and disco lighting simply were not for her. She soon left the evening, and I did not see her again. After speaking to Sarah, I felt that she had a rather unique experience of the community and would provide a valuable contribution to this study. Unfortunately, after various unsuccessful attempts to contact her, I can only conclude that she did not want to take part in this research.

If, as Sarah and Jenny describe, the vampire community does not provide the cultural aspects that they seek, and therefore they must find these pleasures elsewhere (Jenny indicates that she frequents the Dracula Society, which is a more traditional literary fan community), questions must be raised concerning the nature of the fan community. If, for so many, the attractions are increasingly tied to socializing, drinking, music, and dress, what is left for a vampire community that is emptied of its meaning? Is it about the vampire at all? Or is it merely an identity subculture? Perhaps a closer look at vampire style might assist in answering this question.

VAMPIRE DRESS AND CREATIVITY

Before addressing this issue of the vampire community and its (thus far) seemingly loose connection with the vampire legend, this section will first begin with an explanation of how members of the community dress. As the following section will reveal, it is only by accounting for the types of clothes worn by women and the inspirations used within their outfits that we can begin to understand the complex relationship between the community and the vampire. Contrary to the evidence produced in the previous section, vampire dress does reveal that women may be fans of the vampire after all.

Lifestylers and Ritual Dressers

Dressing in vampire fashion is an extremely important aspect of vampire community lifestyle; however, the extent and frequency that members fashion the vampire is wide ranging (see Figure 3). Data suggest that over half of the community dress in a vampire style of clothing as part of their everyday lifestyle (57 percent). These women continue to fashion alternative, sartorial identities on a full-time basis, in all aspects of life, wearing their vampire dress at home, to work, and to social events within and outside of the subculture, often discussing how they may have to curtail their outfits for practicalities, such as cycling to work, but wearing full makeup, corsetry, and blacks, purples, reds and, in some instances, fangs, as part of their everyday attire.

Alternatively, 36 percent of the community are more ritualistic dressers, who dress up for vampire-related events only. These women tend to be governed by segregated audiences, performing varying and at times conflicting identities in different contexts. These more ritualistic dressers use the vampire community as an escapist pleasure, so that they can dress differently to the more conventional styles they wear in everyday life. Some members discuss how they might consciously conceal their vampire fashion (i.e., the fact that they engage in vampire dress practices at all) from the other aspects of their life, such as work and partners. Others are more open about their participation but prefer to keep it separate for reasons of time,

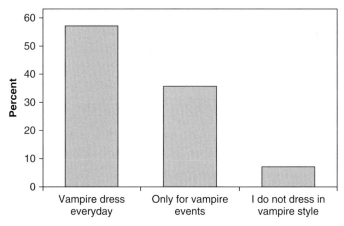

Figure 3 Bar chart of vampire dress

practicalities, expense, or simply because they enjoy the carnivalesque outlet (Bakhtin 1968) and the chance to play and experiment in a form of "temporary liberation" (1968: 34).

> VC10: I have a very vivid imagination and enjoy vampire fantasy. I like to be around others who think the same. Life is so conventional and boring at times, it is great to have an outlet where people can go and express their innermost and darkest desires without fear of judgement. (VC10, Questionnaire)

For other women, it appears to be about expressing their identity in a way they aspire to in everyday life. These women are often limited to more conventional dress practices because of time limitations or personal and work obligations that prevent them from engaging in more alternative performances. These women often have two wardrobes, and they select from both, pairing their work clothes with an assortment of lace, frills, jewelry, and black makeup and nail polish where possible. For instance, Rebecca, the London Vampyre Group social secretary, discussed that her job in the city places certain restriction on her clothing, as she feels that vampire dress is not acceptable and she must adhere to more corporate codes of dress. However, she does attempt to combine her vampire interests with her working wardrobe when possible: "I will often sneak a touch of alternative into the outfit, be it platform knee-length boots, a corset, or a crucifix" (Rebecca, Group Interview 1).

There was also a very small proportion of the community who, while filling out the questionnaire, chose the "I do not dress up in vampire/alternative clothing" option (7 percent). On closer inspection, the remainder of their questionnaire answers included descriptions such as, "I dress with a hint of the gothic," and "mostly wearing black" that appeared at odds with their first statement. My own observations of these women revealed that although they were less inclined to fully commit to fashioning the vampire, they wore mostly black and fashioned some gothic-inspired jewelry. On the whole, this small fragment may be less involved in fashioning vampire style, but they feel compelled to fit in with the wider aesthetic of the group (chapter 6 explores issues of this type of forced sartorial conformity in more detail).

Vampire Clothes and Accessories

The garments worn by respondents are extremely diverse and are purchased from a range of alternative shops, both online and on the high street, including The Dark Side, Mrs. Hippy, Gootik, Drac-in-a-Box, Fairy Goth Mother, Laughing Vampire, and Camden's Stables Market. Members also shop at vintage fairs, charity shops, secondhand clothes shops, and eBay as well as purchasing items from high-street retailers such as H&M, Top Shop, and Zara, which they then customize. The most popular items that respondents listed on the questionnaire include black clothes, lace/velvet tops, dark eyeliner, dark nail polish, corsets, fishnet stockings, dark lipstick, silver jewelry, gloves, bustled skirts, crucifixes, chokers and wrist cuffs, and custom-made fangs. Respondents also state that they sport tattoos and body piercings.

Garments that are less popular with respondents include pairing jeans and corsets (only 3 percent of the community do this), boot covers, goth blood, combat trousers, and fashion contact lenses. The rejection of garments such as combat trousers and boot covers, which are more modern and could even be considered as unisex styles, may suggest that the community is selecting more feminine clothes, such as lace/velvet tops, fishnets, and corsets (a theme that will be developed during the next chapter). Similarly, respondents' lack of interest in fake blood, fashion contact lenses, and pairing historical clothes with more conventional fashion (e.g., jeans) may also suggests that women are maintaining a level of authenticity to a specific time period rather than attempting to dress up.

Through both my observations of the community and the most frequently listed items on the questionnaire, it is apparent that the vampire community has their own identifiable vampire look, which comprises a highly feminine, romantic, historical (usually late Victorian) style of dress that is black or dark in color. However, on the whole, women's wardrobes are extremely eclectic, and members fashion styles from wider subcultures. For instance, retro fashions,

S&M, steampunk, corporate goth, and elegant gothic Lolita (EGL)[5] are also used as inspiration for outfits. This diversity reveals a wider and more general breakdown in the distinction between alternative communities, as women can wear full Victorian mourning costume, complete with fangs, veil, and corset, to one event and then fashion a steampunk Girl Genius[6] outfit with miniskirt and brass driving goggles and compass to the next (see Figures 4–7). This eclecticism and general bricolage of subcultural aesthetics has been identified by the London Vampyre Group's fanzine, *Chronicles*, which has a regular, full-color centerfold each issue that explores a different member's wardrobe, ironically titled "Goths! They just wear black don't they?"

Figures 4–7 Subcultural bricolage: Images of Rebecca in steampunk, vampire, "trad goth," and Elizabethan outfits. Photographs: Soulstealer Photography (SoulStealer.co.uk)

Vampire film and television also informs women's outfits. For example, although women have shown an interest in films with more contemporary settings, such as *Blade* and *The Lost Boys*, the historical vampire is the most popular type of vampire film (74 percent of women selected this type of vampire as their favorite). The "stunning historical costumes" (Rebecca, Group Interview 1) of "well dressed" vampires (LVG5, Questionnaire) and gothic set designs have been noted as reasons for their viewing pleasure, with *Interview with the Vampire* ranking most highly, closely followed by *Bram Stoker's Dracula* and *Queen of the Damned*.[7]

The costumes worn by these historical vampire characters have been reperformed by women. Examples include the black lace mask and gothic choker worn by Sylvia (Monica Bellucci) in *Brotherhood of the Wolf*, the gothic Lolita-style dress worn by Mina (Winona Ryder) in *Bram Stoker's Dracula,* and the full costume of Queen Akasha (Aaliyah) worn in *Queen of the Damned* (see Figures 8 and 9). More modern vampire film and television styles have also informed women's sartorial choices, including hairstyles, such as *The Lost Boys* white crop, worn by Jenny, and the recent *True Blood*–inspired outfit that was worn by Nancy to the Blood Lust: Southern Vampire Party. However, although vampire and gothic cinema may influence women, they are doing more than costuming or wearing their fandom.

Women are not dressing up as characters in the narrative or reenacting period costume. In contrast, women are incorporating a vampire aesthetic into their wider fashion style, borrowing from aspects of celluloid vampire for the outfits they wear at meetings and events. So while there are some rare exceptions of women imitating styles from films and television programs, these extra textual features are then transformed into a wider sense of self

Figure 8 Vampire media inspiration: Nancy as *True Blood*'s Sookie Stackhouse, Southern Vampire Party. Photograph: Soulstealer Photography (SoulStealer.co.uk)

Figure 9   Vampire media inspiration: *Queen of the Damned*, Vampyre Villains versus Steampunk Slayers Costume Showdown Party. Photograph: Soulstealer Photography (SoulStealer. co.uk)

and incorporated into their own vampire identity, thereby taking the cult outside of the cinema. For example, when asked about influences on their dress, participants responded with various examples from popular culture. They suggested that they were not influenced by a specific person, character or trend, but instead integrated a host of influences into their wider style.

> Nancy: I am trying to imitate a hairdo I saw on the *Moonlight* series right now.
> Lou: I think everything influences me really. . . . I would like to look like Immodesty Blaize, the UK Dita Von Teese, I love Burlesque looks. I think Kate Beckinsale is stunning in *Van Helsing*.
> Lyla[8]: I tend to go through historical periods. I like Edwardian and Victorian times. They were much nicer, although it did take a lot longer to get dressed! (Group Interview 1)

Therefore, going back to the question raised at the end of the last section, concerning the somewhat precarious nature of the fan community, a closer inspection of women's dress reveals that the community's interests in the vampire are actually thoroughly maintained through members' creative practices, as the community exists as both a fandom and a subculture. Though they may not need to engage in fully fledged intellectual debates about the vampire on a regular basis, their interests in history, the vampire, and the gothic are all transformed into highly visual lifestyle commodities, as they immerse themselves in their interests in everyday life. This relationship is far more complex and sophisticated than simply dressing up as vampire characters. Whether in the form of presenting their own alternative pseudohistorical version of London (as demonstrated by the Victorian pub crawl in the previous chapter) or by wandering around a graveyard and immersing themselves in the aesthetics of morbidity, women are reimagining the vampire within their own lives.

As Henry Jenkins describes in his seminal work *Textual Poachers: Television Fans and Participatory Culture* (1992), the principles of fandom are much like the children's story *The Velveteen Rabbit*. During the story, the old Skin Horse offers the Velveteen Rabbit a lecture, explaining that "when a child really loves you for a long, long time, not just to play with, but REALLY loves you, then you become real" (Bianco 1983, in Jenkins 1992: 50). In a similar vein, the community's fascination for the vampire and wider gothic culture also transforms it into the real, giving it new meaning, as the vampire is integrated into their imaginative experiences. As the following section continues to reveal, women participate with the vampire, and even poach from vampire texts, in a number of different and highly creative ways.

Wider Productivity and Microeconomies

As well as demonstrating their creativity by assembling vampire outfits, vampire community members also engage in wider forms of visual expression and fan productivity. For example, evidence suggests that just under half of members in the community have created their own vampire fan fiction. These fictions include short stories, novels, e-books (available on sites such as fictionpress.com), poetry, vampire artwork, vampire body art, digitally manipulated photography, and articles in both *Chronicles* and *Dark Nights* fanzines. Specific examples of the fan fictions described by respondents include a collection of short stories based on childhood dreams about vampires, and one respondent has also created her own comic strip in the style of *Dogwitch*, which is about a witch-superstar who was previously a lead singer in a rock band and now summons demons and vampires.

As Sarah Thornton's research alludes (see chapter 3), a range of subcultural businesses have also emerged within the vampire community, as members have extended their production of fan fiction to more professional

Figures 10–11 Creative productivity: Jewelry and accessories. Photographs: Enlyl's Realm

Figures 12–13 Creative productivity: Filmmaking and modeling. Photographs: Soulstealer Photography (SoulStealer.co.uk). Vampire short film to promote the launch of the book *Bite: A Vampire Handbook*, by Kevin Jackson

undertakings and have managed to capitalize on their interests in the vampire. For example, Nancy has recently published her first book, titled *Take a Bite*, with Callio Press, which traces the vampire through folklore and fiction. Although Nancy is not in a position to become a professional full-time author and works in healthcare administration, in her spare time she has also begun to attend academic conferences on vampires and wider occult literature, and she recently presented a paper titled "Women with Bite: Tracing Vampire Women from Lilith to *Twilight*" at the Vampires: Myths of the Past and Future conference at the University of London.

Wider examples of vampire fan productivity also include the production of vampire, gothic, and steampunk jewelry and accessories, which community members are increasingly using to generate extra income revenues, as they sell their designs to other community members online and at vampire events. For example, Audrey creates her own handmade jewelry and accessories, which she then advertises on her Facebook, MySpace, and LiveJournal profiles (see Figures 10 and 11). Community members can browse her designs, see images of her modeling her arts and crafts, and then follow the click-through to etsy.com,[9] where Audrey has set up her online shop—Enlyl's Realm: Gothic Fantasies and Steampunk Inventions. Community members can also take part in professional/semiprofessional photo shoots, as photographers, makeup artists, and models. The photographs are then sold to magazines, such as *Nocturnal Magazine*, used in the community fanzines, or displayed on women's social media sites as part of their alternative modeling portfolios (see Figures 12 and 13).

As these highly creative and, in some cases, professional practices reveal, the vampire community is increasingly collapsing the boundaries between traditional science fiction and fantasy fan cultures with its intellectual pursuit, and the more performative subcultures, as essentially the community exists as a combination of the two. Through dress and wider productivity, community members maintain their intellectual interests in the historical and vampire media (i.e., fan object) but transform their fan interests into clothing and the performance of a vampire identity.

VAMPIRE MEDIA

Finally, it is important to establish the community's consumption of vampire media. As previously discussed, community members do not spend the majority of their time critiquing and debating vampire fiction; however, they do consume a wide variety of media, which provide important insights into community life. As the following section reveals, women's fictional tastes continue to demonstrate shared values among the community, including a fascination with the historical and themes of the heterosexual romance.

True Blood: Twilight for Grown-Ups?

The majority of interview and questionnaire research for this book was carried out over the three-year period of 2006 to 2009, but smaller scale participant observations, retrospective interviews, and questionnaires continued up until 2012. Therefore, vast amounts of this data were collected prior to the recent vampire craze that was documented in the opening chapter, brought about by the widespread popularity of television and film releases, such as *Twilight*, *True Blood*, *Vampire Diaries*, *Let the Right One In*, and *Being Human*.[10] Although I cannot attempt to quantify the popularity of these recent examples of vampire media as I have with other popular fictions (see the following section on tastes), retrospective interviews and my own conversations with members of the community reveals that these new vampire installments (*True Blood*, in particular) are being consumed. In fact, *True Blood*, together with *Twilight* and *Interview with the Vampire*, inspired an entire London Vampyre Group event, Blood Lust: Southern Vampire Party, in 2010. The flier for the event asked members: "Are you an Edward or Bella from Arizona? Bill or Sookie from Bon Temps? Lestat from New Orleans? Then you are in excellent company as the theme is good ole Southern Vampires" (LVG Website, vampyregroup.co.uk).

While *Twilight* has received an extremely mixed response from members of the vampire community, *True Blood*, with its hard-hitting, gritty, sexy, and particularly bloody vampire appeal has experienced extensive popularity among members. Despite minor complaints about the highly gratuitous portrayal of sex and violence within the show, with one member suggesting it was "all sex and no story" (Mel, Questionnaire), on the whole, interviews revealed that it was precisely the adult content of Alan Ball's series that was celebrated by the vampire community. *True Blood* was repeatedly praised by members for its hard-hitting nature, a feature that was made even more appealing in the midst of other, more muted vampire texts, such as *Twilight* and *Vampire Diaries*. *True Blood* was frequently referred to as *Twilight* for grown-ups, as women frequently pitted these franchises against each other. Even when women enjoyed both texts, they often referred to the adult nature of *True Blood* and communicated their pleasure in the inclusion of such gritty, provocative material.

One respondent commented that *True Blood*'s vampires are "more real and dangerous," and "they don't sparkle" (Jenni, Questionnaire). As this community member highlights, *Twilight*'s sparkly vampires are a key identifying feature of the *True Blood* versus *Twilight* opposition, which has been picked up more widely through the production of "real vampires don't sparkle" anti-*Twilight* T-shirts, which are available at various online retailers.

Another potentially attractive feature of *True Blood* that was identified by members of the vampire community is the alternative outsider status of its central characters. Numerous members of the community stated that they particularly enjoyed the theme of the outsider, portrayed through characters such as Lafayette and Tara. Sookie was also specifically noted as an outsider, as she does not fit into the wider Bon Temps community. From the first episode of the television series, Sookie is referred to as *freak*, and being as *crazy as a bed bug* due her telepathic *disability* (*True Blood* 1:1). However, as the narrative unfolds, Sookie is revealed to be a character of great emotional and physical strength, and her insertion into the supernatural world allows her to fit into an alternative community of people who are different. Sookie, like the other *supes*, is presented as unusual and unique. For instance, Lou suggests that she finds this extremely positive treatment of outsider characters within *True Blood* particularly appealing. She states that the outsider theme can also be noted across wider vampire fictions, such as *Twilight*, and considers that there are similar pleasures to be found in both consuming vampire media and belonging to alternative groups such as the vampire community.

> Lou: Bella and Sookie, both see themselves as kind of misfits, and the supernatural world offers them a place to belong. Bella turns out to be a very capable vampire, so she finally finds something she is good at. Sookie finds people weirder than her that value her gift so she is not an outcast for it. . . . Maybe recent vampire fictions are validating and "ok-ing" being outsiders, misfits (emo kids, goths). These groups are suddenly finding themselves cool and "in"—if you are a bit different that is fine. (Louisa, Retrospective Interview)

Therefore, in general, the vampire community does seem to be riding the current vampire wave, as they are embracing, as opposed to resisting, the coverage of vampires in the mainstream. However, some members have suggested that when the mainstream get bored of vampires, the hard-core fans (i.e., members of the vampire community) will remain faithful to vampire fiction, as they are the more devoted and authentic audience. Lucy sums up this attitude when she states that she is currently "taking great advantage of all the book re-releases," but realizes that "when the hype dies down, it will leave just us hard core. We will go back to desperately waiting for the next vampire film that has more than a £100 budget to come out" (Lucy, Questionnaire).

Tastes

Alongside the popularity of recent vampire installments such as *True Blood*, members consume a broad range of vampire media. During the questionnaire, members were invited to list their favorite vampire film or television show. These were particularly wide-ranging and included *Queen of the Damned*, *Bram Stoker's Dracula*, *Buffy the Vampire Slayer*, *The Hunger*, *Nosferatu*, *The Lost Boys*, *Underworld*, *Ultraviolet* (television series), *Interview with the Vampire*, and *Blade.* The variation in titles suggests that the vampire community does not form a close association with one specific vampire text (i.e., it is not predominantly made up of Buffy fans), although the most popular film was *Interview with the Vampire*, followed by *The Lost Boys*, and *Bram Stoker's Dracula.*

With the exception of *The Lost Boys*, the two most popular films are period inspired, and given the nature of women's historical dress practices could therefore suggest a link between the community and a preference for onscreen historical aesthetics, but these results are far from conclusive. The popularity of these films is more likely to be attributed to the quality of their production and the timing of their release in the late 1980s and early 1990s. Taking into consideration that the majority of women are in their twenties and thirties, respondents would have been in their teenage years when these films were released. Therefore, interest in the films may also be associated with women's adolescence, a time to which many respondents have linked their interests in the vampire. For instance, when respondents were invited to state what first attracted them to vampires, responses included, "I found vampires very sensual and erotic from a young age" (LVG17, Questionnaire), "I have loved vampires and the spooky since childhood" (VC18, Questionnaire), and "my interests go back to when I first started reading about Vlad the Impaler in history in Junior school" (LVG34, Questionnaire).

When respondents were invited to state their favorite type of vampire, evidence is more conclusive in suggesting that women have a preference for historical aesthetics in vampire media, as although the question was open ended, women's responses were surprisingly similar and fit into rather narrow categories. They consist of the male historical, the male romantic, the female historical, and the general historical. It is evident that the majority of responses were associated with a particularly Mills & Boon[11] style of romantic heterosexual fantasy, as respondents described a strong, historical male vampire paired with a beautiful female.

Women repeatedly wrote responses, such as "my perfect vampire is a male stereotypical vampire in historical frock coat, well dressed and charming" (LVG5, Questionnaire), "tall sexy ancient Roman, Greek or Atlantean vampires" (LVG6, Questionnaire), "historical gorgeous male" (LVMG7, Questionnaire), "male dominant and passive aggressive sexy female" (VC10, Questionnaire), "male Victorian type" (VC11, Questionnaire), "male historical" (LVG12, Questionnaire), "romantic, dark brooding, seductive male" (VC15, Questionnaire), "straight male handsome" (LVMG26, Questionnaire), and "smart Victorian men and women in beautiful full dresses—self-aware" (VC27, Questionnaire). Even responses to more recent vampire fictions with much more contemporary settings, such as *Twilight* and *True Blood*, continued to allude to the importance of the heterosexual romance theme, as women particularly enjoyed romantic narratives between Eric and Sookie in *True Blood* and Edward and Bella in *Twilight*.

When respondents were asked to list their favorite vampire character, themes of the historical continued, as respondents most frequently listed historical male vampires as opposed to modern male vampires, such as Blade, or female vampires, such as Queen Akasha from *Queen of the Damned*. Respondents' favorite vampire is Lestat, closely followed by Dracula. Other popular vampires include Louis and Armand from Anne Rice's *Interview with the Vampire* and Spike from *Buffy the Vampire Slayer*. Respondents did list some female vampires, such as Claudia from *Interview with the Vampire*, Miriam from *The Hunger*, and Elizabeth Bathory, but the majority of responses were male and historical.

Therefore, as respondents' tastes and viewing practices reveal, women's attachment to the vampire appears to be associated with an interest in the historical and with a particularly heterosexual romance fantasy, a theme that will be explored in detail throughout the following chapter.

SUMMARY

Going back to the picture that is emerging of the female vampire community member, we have already established that she is likely to be in her late twenties or early thirties, heterosexual, well educated, and white. She may have originally joined the community to experience something out of the ordinary and to meet new people, or through her wider immersion in another alternative community, such as goth culture. She may now attend a host of the community's social events and is likely to spend a degree of her time socializing with other vampire club members at monthly gatherings as well as at organized events, such as Vampyre Villains versus Steampunk Slayers Costume Showdown Party, and Southern Vampire themed parties, where she will almost certainly fashion a vampire/historical style.

Her outfits are eclectic and might include inspiration from wider alternative communities, such as steampunk and BDSM fetish wear, but they will more than likely include a host of black garments, lace/velvet tops, dark eyeliner, dark nail polish, corsetry, and, in some instances, fangs. She may either dress this way on a daily basis or only for specifically related vampire events. As well as reimagining the vampire through clothes, she may also engage in the production of wider vampire-related commodities, from vampire-inspired artwork to running her own small jewelry business. She may enjoy reading vampire books and watching vampire television and films and is predominantly interested in the male historical vampire, but her tastes are not limited to this, as she may also enjoy female vampires and more modern looking vampire media, such as *The Lost Boys*, *Twilight*, and *True Blood*.

Having presented a descriptive profile of the vampire community and addressed one of the key research questions that is concerned with *how* vampire culture is fashioned and commodified by members of the community, the discussion will now move on to explore in more detail issues that have arisen in this chapter. The following pages will consider women's historical, heterosexual, and particularly feminine response to the vampire and will ask *why* women choose to adorn themselves in clothes and lifestyle accessories that reimagine a morbid past.

–5–

Feminine Discourses

It is the final Thursday of the month, and once again I find myself fighting my way onto the London underground during rush hour, ready to attend the Vampyre Connexion monthly social at the Blue Posts pub, Soho. On this occasion, I have decided to invite my sister. Although she is not an active member of goth or vampire scenes, she has always had a penchant for gothic clothes and music (particularly in her teens and early twenties). As it is her first time out on the vampire circuit, I have brought some back issues of *Chronicles* fanzine, in order to explain the subculture in a bit more detail. We begin to flick through the pages, and come across an article titled "Are We R.O.A.Ring Loud Enough" (Daynes 2007). The article examines acceptable codes of dress for vampire community events and more specifically the community's policy to exercise its Right of Admission Refusal, so that it can deter unwanted, inappropriately attired guests. The author explains her frustrations over the "infiltration" of community events by people who would look more at home in an R&B club or "poncy" wine bar. The article specifies people who should be forcibly removed from alternative venues, including "anyone in sportswear" and "girls that think that buying an off-the-peg PVC dress makes them a goth for the night," especially when it's paired with a blonde ponytail and neutral makeup (Daynes 2007: 42).

Although the article is written in a tongue-in-cheek style and certainly does not represent the attitudes of all members of the vampire community (the majority of women would like to see people making an effort but do not necessarily want to forcibly remove those who attend in less alternative clothes), it did prompt a last-minute darkening of my own eyeliner and a quick check of my blonde hair, which thankfully was not styled in a ponytail that evening. Although I continue to feel more at ease at vampire events, I am still in the process of trying to break into groups of friends that have been attending for much longer and who share similar interests in clothes, music, and lifestyle activities. Consequently, I am constantly taking steps to avoid any outward signs that might be deemed antagonistic or disrespectful to the wider community. With my concerns about my appearance appeased, and safe in the knowledge that my sister's style was more naturally akin to the general tastes of the group— with her long dark hair, pale complexion, striking makeup, body art, and black clothes—we arrived at the Blue Posts and made our way to the upstairs private room.

We stood at the entrance, where a small table had been arranged with a register so that members could sign in and make a contribution. I glanced around to see who was in attendance this evening. There was MorbidFrog, raising a pint of stout to her fanged mouth. She was wearing a black and red corset with a skeleton and rose print, and a long dark skirt that gathered in a bustle at the back. She had several tattoos and had stenciled a mask of black ivy swirls across her cheekbones and lower forehead; her long, black, wavy hair trailed the bottom of her back. She was chatting to Audrey, who was wearing an elegant gothic Lolita (EGL) style mini dress, with long socks. Her low-cut neckline allowed her to show off her new brooch piercing (she wore a delicate diamond in her upper chest). Jenny, the figurehead of the Vampyre Connexion, was wearing a long, black lace and velvet dress with short veil. She was standing with her husband, Vampire Master Colin, who was dressed in a black frock coat, cravat, and long black ponytail. Together they warmly received members as they arrived, with Jenny introducing new members to the wider social circle while Colin bowed down to kiss their hands and exchange pleasantries.

Once we had signed in, I left my sister with the bags and coats and joined the bar queue. After negotiating a very small space with a woman in a very generous crinoline, I bought the drinks and made my way back to my sister, who by now appeared to be a little overwhelmed. She told me that in my absence she had felt a little conspicuous and had therefore decided to have a cigarette to fill the time until I returned. She was fumbling around in her pocket for a lighter, when a "devastatingly handsome gentleman" seemed to emerge out of the darkness, clad in black frock coat, with long dark hair and dark brooding eyes. He gazed straight into her eyes, slowly leant in and lit her cigarette, smiled, revealing two fanged teeth, and then vanished as quickly as he arrived; he did this all without saying a word.

Although an outsider, my sister's retelling of her encounter with the chivalrous and alluring vampire member, which left her positively swooning, resembled the romantic, almost Mills & Boon appeal of the vampire that had been expressed by so many members of the vampire community. As the previous chapter revealed, the appeal of the vampire appears to be linked with the appeal of male dominance and female submission, or what Dracula actor Frank Langella has referred to as the "white horse" effect. During an interview with *Playboy* Magazine, Langella proposed that "vampires are sexy to a woman perhaps because the fantasy is similar to that of the man on the white horse sweeping her off to paradise" (Rosen 1979).[1]

That evening's encounter, alongside the numerous statements made by vampire community members that revealed a preoccupation with romantic and historical themes, made me start questioning the nature of the vampire community and just what it offers to women. Although, as the *Chronicles* article reveals, dress clearly is an extremely important factor of community life, I realized that the vampire community offers members more than the opportunity to fashion vampire clothes and lifestyle, as it also appears to provide some kind of historical vampire fantasy in a real-world context. I wanted to establish just what was underneath these extremely feminine, romantic performances.

Further, while I was sure that these feminine identity performances were common among vampire community members, I also wanted to explore those experiences that did not fit so neatly into this reading—as conversations with vampire members revealed that the cult of femininity (Brill 2008) did not extend to *all* members. Like any group of people, the vampire community is not a cohesive space, with all women experiencing vampire culture in the same way, but instead reveals a diversity of styles and tastes, which also highlight opposing and contradictory experiences. For instance, although many women use vampire dress to adorn themselves in excessively feminine clothes, others use vampire clothes to fashion androgyny. Similarly, the gothic vampire ideal of pale white skin, framed with long black hair is a popular look with many community members, but mixed-race vampire community members experience an altogether different type of beauty aesthetic, devoid of this trademark pale complexion.

This chapter therefore focuses on the predominant underlying discourses of the vampire community and how women represent their values and feelings about gender through the discussion and topics around which they center. Essentially, four discourses have emerged from the data, which reveal the often-varied experiences of community membership. These include the romanticization of the past, excessive femininity, androgyny and variation, and identification and outsiderdom,[2] and will now be investigated in detail.

ROMANTICIZATION OF THE PAST

The romanticization of the past discourse was particularly evident throughout this research, as the vampire community continued to discuss a fascination with the historical, and particularly the Victorian period, that has clearly influenced their dress practices. An overwhelming number of women who took part in this study revealed a romantic fascination with the gothic that goes back to childhood. For example, when filling out the questionnaire, participants were asked the open-ended question, "What first attracted you to vampires?" In response, 80 percent of participants specifically identified their interest in vampires as dating back to the literature they read as children, or having "always" been interested in vampires. Women described vampires as agents of seduction, who were "attractive" (Ronita, Individual Interview 1) and "beautiful creatures" (VC27, Questionnaire), telling stories about how they " 'fell in love" (LVMG7, Questionnaire) with vampires, even during their childhood, particularly coinciding with puberty. Women discussed how their love for the vampire formed part of a wider interest in gothic activities, visiting church graveyards, cathedrals, theaters, and the Victoria and Albert Museum, and a general affinity with the Victorian period from a young age. Jenny, the previous Vampyre Connexion organizer, identifies her interest in the gothic as dating back to her childhood. She discusses her particular interest in a romantic gothic aesthetic, revealing her romanticization of historical costumes, describing how she "drooled" over them.

> Jenny: As a child I always loved that kind of thing, I had a great aunt who had a traditional parlour at the front of her house that was only open for funerals. That was a real Victorian room, it had all the stuffed animals, stuffed seals, those traditional china dogs, I used to love that room. I must have had an affinity with the period even as a child. I used to love all the old churches even then, and the V&A Museum. I used to drool over the costumes, the wonderful bustles. (Individual Interview 2)

As adults, this romanticization of the historical can also be mapped to women's online activities, as members' social media profiles demonstrate an anachronistic fusion between past and present. For example, profiles often privilege a historic, quite often Victorian, aesthetic, but use new technologies, such as posting videos, digital photography, and music clips to do so. Video postings include personal footage of the members of the Brighton and London Vampyre Group's outing to the Bluebell Railway (a heritage steam railway in Sussex) as well as clips of women in full Victorian dress walking through Nunhead Cemetery. Similarly, one participant's Facebook profile includes an album titled An Outfit in the Making, which displays various scanned images of her own historical dressmaking process. These include early pencil sketching and designs of the period costume, photos of the dress in varying stages of completion, and images of her wearing it to Sarabande (historical dance).

Figure 14   Reimagining the historical. Photograph: Soulstealer Photography (SoulStealer.co.uk)

Similarly, the imported media clips that are uploaded on members' pro-file pages also reveal a level of anachronism. Profiles contain videos ex-hibiting a collection of silent black-and-white films from the early twentieth century (e.g., *Nosferatu*), to more modern music videos with a historical/ vampire aesthetic. For example, fan-made videos such as "Vampire Per-fect Skin" have been uploaded, which is a re-edited version of the music video *Perfect Skin*, by 69 Eyes, to include clips from the film *Queen of the Damned*, based on Anne Rice's novel of the same name. There are also an assortment of sound tracks and theme tunes on profiles, ranging from art-ists such as Marilyn Manson, Inkubus Sukkubus, and Theatre des Vampires that are associated with the subculture, to classical theme tunes such as Mozart's *Requiem*. Digital photography includes images of women in an array of gothic/vampire-inspired outfits, photographs and imagery of pre-Raphaelite paintings and sculptures, and more negotiated images of women in digitally modified poses. These typically include images of women in full gothic vampire costume, simulating "the bite" (as exemplified by Jenny); Japanese Lolita-inspired poses (as demonstrated by Audrey); and more medieval, ethereal images of vampiric flower fairies with digitally mastered wings (as illustrated by MorbidFrog).

Online profiles also reveal historical objects associated with paganism, with some women selecting Wicca to guide their religious views and displaying various Wiccan/occult iconography, such as pentagram graphics. For example, Lyla's Facebook profile reveals that she is a member of groups such as the Sevenoaks Spiritual Awareness Centre, Beelzebub Sabbath Church, Pentacle Media, and the UK Paranormal Network. Her profile displays images of witch pendants, historical goblets, fairies, and various other aesthetics associated with Wicca. She has also downloaded applications such as Altar Gifts for Witches, Magical Creatures, Pagan Presents, Fairies, and Witchy Stuff. In the about me section, she states, "I am a young at heart gothic alternative Wiccan . . . and love to walk in cemeteries and down by the water." This highlights that the allure Lyla finds in ancient Wiccan spirituality is also linked to fascination in the gothic and the historical.

Therefore, Facebook profiles can reveal eclectic mixtures of histories that merge a variety of historical trends but are not necessarily faithful to any one particular time period. As women use the application of modern technologies such as video postings and digital manipulation software to galvanize a neo-Victorian lifestyle online, modifying and re-mapping their favorite imagined histories or "modding"[3] the past, they are drawing on their favorite historical aesthetics (e.g., images of a steam train) and using new technologies to modify and reimagine those histories.

STEAMPUNK

Another particularly significant example of the vampire community's anachronistic pleasures is the community's recent fascination with the steampunk movement, and particularly with steamfashion. Steampunk originated as a literary subgenre; it has roots in Victorian fictions, such as Jules Verne's *Twenty Thousand Leagues Under the Sea* (1869) and H. G. Wells's *The Time Machine* (1895), to more specifically labeled steampunk literature, such as

Tim Powers's *The Anubis Gates* (1983) and, more recently, Philip Pullman's *His Dark Materials* trilogy (1995–2000). Steampunk is a particularly visual form of fiction, organized around steam-driven advanced science and technology, anachronistically retrofitted onto a Victorian-themed world. Due in a large part to this visual quality, it has translated easily into other media such as film, television, comic books, and video games. The appeal of steampunk's anachronistic visual aesthetic has extended the pleasures of steampunk from traditional consumption activities to those associated with production. Moreover, due to steampunk's popularity with various fan and style communities, not least in the subgenre's close links with the science fiction fan communities (e.g., steam *Star Wars* and steam *Dr. Who*) and its particularly active and productive fans, steampunk has evolved into a performative style subculture associated with recognizable fashions and lifestyle accessories. The recent feature in the London Vampyre Group's fanzine *Chronicles* describes the movement as follows:

> Imagine what at first seems to be a group of people dressed in Victorian clothing. However, here lace gives way to leather, trousers are tucked into heavyweight boots and top hats have forsaken their hatbands in favour of Brassgoggles. Complex looking scientific devices are their decoration and airships fill the air. Welcome to the world of Steampunk. (Sadeian 2008: 10)

As the feature goes on to outline, the very nature of steampunk lies in its anachronism, the focus being on "period inspired," not "period re-enacted" dress (2008: 10). Since 2006, steampunk style has trickled-across (to borrow a term from King [1963]) to the vampire community, as numerous members have revealed an increasing interest in steampunk or variations on the theme, such as steamgoth. The vampire community's adoption of aspects of steampunk lifestyle range from the adoption of steampunk objects, both online and through women's dress practices, to members' attendance of specifically organized steampunk events, such as Vampyre Villains versus Steampunk Slayers Costume Showdown party (organized by the London Vampyre Group) and White Mischief, which is a series of themed evenings that include events such as From the Earth to the Moon and Around the World in 80 Days, with historical activities such as vaudeville, phantasmagoria, snake charming, and low-voltage electrocution.

As the following statement by Jenny articulates, the community's adoption of steampunk aesthetics can be viewed as a natural evolution in vampire style, continuing their interest in Victorian, Edwardian, and other historical periods:

Jenny: I have always been interested in the Victorian/Edwardian period, with bustled skirts and riding jackets. I have several real Victorian capes, Victorian drape bustle skirts, loads of corsets . . . I have recently just started getting into steampunk. Having got the *League of Extraordinary Gentlemen* amongst other things, I suddenly realized I quite like that Victorian steampunky kind of thing. There is also a steampunk forum online that I have just started getting into. (Individual Interview 2)

As Jenny highlights, the vampire community use online forums and social media sites to inform their steampunk style. For example, during interviews, participants discussed visiting the steampunk website Brassgoggles[4] and LiveJournal's Steamfashion community[5] to get fashion tips and insider knowledge, so that they could then create their own steampunk outfits. The growth in online communities has clearly played an integral role in the diffusion of the style across the vampire community, providing a visual dialogue between members.

Rebecca: I use the LiveJournal Steamfashion site for fashion. This is how LiveJournal works; its insider knowledge. People on the forum describe things in such detail; it's how you can get ideas. (Group Interview 1)

Having gained "insider knowledge" from social media and created their steampunk outfits, women can then contribute to the dialogue by posting their own images of anachronistic steamfashions. From these images and the observations conducted at vampire/steampunk events, it was evident that styles comprise a selection of bloomers, corsets, high-neck shirts, cropped trousers, long skirts, and spats. Styles were teamed with gadgetry, such as intricately worked compasses, pocket watches, and various other accessories, such as signature brass motoring goggles, Edwardian lorgnette spectacles, modified guns, cog pendants, decorative turn keys, and deconstructed jewelry made from watch parts.

Even vampire community members who have not yet encountered the movement seem to be drawing on many of its themes unconsciously, often mixing fashions from the past (particularly from the Victorian period) with a more futuristic trend. The focus is on a DIY (do it yourself) style, making your own garments, or at least customizing existing clothes:

Beth: When I make Victorian outfits, sometimes I will embroider them with medieval green and gold. Or if I want to go futuristic I will make Victorian patterns out of PVC, or out of layers of fishnet, or some kind of transparent fabric, but just layered and lined so it's not too modest. The idea being that you see the undergarments, the corset, and the crinoline or the bustle. (Individual Interview 4)

Figure 15   Steampunk style. Photograph: Soulstealer Photography (SoulStealer.co.uk)

Although the styles are extremely diverse, the vampire community's appropriation of the steampunk aesthetic is concerned with the historical, and particularly with fashions from the late Victorian steam era (as opposed to dieselpunk's 1930s and 1940s fashions). However, these styles also reveal that women are not appropriating historical outfits in an attempt to achieve historical verisimilitude; rather, they reimagine outfits from various points in history, but particularly from the late Victorian and Edwardian periods, and then fuse these styles with futuristic science fiction iconography. Therefore, the romanticization of the past discourse reveals that there is a wider community of women interested in vampires that also seem to be interested in the historical, although this relationship is not necessarily as straightforward as it first appears. Women are deliberately embracing the past but do so by imagining alternative histories that are fused with the present and imagined future, and then play these out in a real-world setting.

As well as offering women opportunities to reimagine alternative histories, such anachronistic steampunk displays can also reveal how members of the vampire community experience the present and particularly the current climate of economic, political, and social conflict. First, steampunk's focus on DIY and customization offers practical, cheap alternatives to purchasing new outfits, a theme that is very much in tune with the style ethos of many members of the vampire community, especially amid recent financial hardship. Second, as well as providing ways to extend one's wardrobe at minimal cost, steampunk also promises cathartic escapist scenarios, as the movement is also associated with social mobility and the formation of a class identity. Through steampunk, individuals can be lifted out of their daily lives—where they are inundated with reports of the latest post-credit crunch financial downturn and news stories about social anxiety and disorder exemplified by continual strikes and protests, culminating in the 2011 riots—and be propelled into alternative histories, where they can be members of the upper classes and use airships as their preferred mode of transport. There is a general sense that through these reimagined fantasies, community members are not returning to the past and selecting lower class vagabonds, maids, or laborers for inspiration, but turn specifically to the nobility and luxury.

The following response from Audrey, who had recently begun to dress in a steampunk style and mod her own jewelry out of deconstructed watch parts, reveals that steampunk and the romanticization of the past discourse in general, is not only about creating alternative histories but is also tied to ideologies of class and returning to periods of history that, sartorially speaking, are viewed by many as more interesting and inspirational than our own.

> Audrey: The influences for my jewelry and accessories are all historical. I love to work with brass, silver, and materials with an antique finish. By the time I have finished making an element, it has already transformed, totally. It turns into something I didn't really predict. I studied Art History, and my main influences include Lolita, neo-Victorianism, and steampunk. . . . In steampunk you see people living a lifestyle you are never going to have. I will never be able to afford all that, but I have my own characters and I can be anything—it is not limited by money. . . . That is what I love about it; you can make goggles out of toilet rolls, use a bit of leather here and there, and you end up with something that you could have brought for £100 on eBay. (Individual Interview 5)

EXCESSIVE FEMININITY

When looking more closely at the romanticization of the past discourse, it is evident that in the majority of cases, these pseudohistorical fantasies include a rather specific version of femininity, which can be described as hyperfeminine, or the excessive femininity discourse. For instance, as documented in the previous chapter, this discourse was apparent during discussions about vampire fiction, and particularly women's tendency to read vampire media as a historical romance. Questionnaire responses revealed that although women have shown an interest in more modern-looking films, such as *Blade* and *The Lost Boys*, the historical vampire is the most popular type of vampire. The stunning historical costumes (Rebecca, Group Interview 1) of well dressed (LVG5, Questionnaire) male Victorian type vampires (VC11, Questionnaire), who are romantic, dark brooding, seductive (VC15, Questionnaire) have been noted as reasons for their viewing pleasure, with *Interview with the Vampire* ranking most highly.

Interviews revealed that when describing the feminine desires of consuming romantic narratives in vampire media, dress appears to be the taxonomy of choice. As Rebecca demonstrates during the following extract, women communicate their pleasure in taking part in a fantasy and falling passively victim to a strong male vampire in terms of appearance and dress. She describes the vampire in historical frock coat, or waistcoat, with long hair, who is "well dressed" and "charming," but "darkly brooding", while the woman is dressed in period corsetry with gaping necklines and long, sweeping skirts that accentuate her femininity.

> Rebecca: I like my vampires to be very strong, almost Mills & Boon, with the trousers and the flowing white shirt, long black hair, and the waistcoat. I love the whole thing, the evil horrid creatures, but my dream vampire is the strong beautiful young male vampire. (Group Interview 1)

This extremely feminine fantasy response highlights a complex negotiation that appears to be occurring with regard to submission and control. The following discussion is particularly useful in highlighting this tension, as women discuss their fantasy of being overpowered by a male vampire, even describing the siring as an "acceptable rape fantasy." This excessive feminine response is juxtaposed with a discussion of women's strong feminine principles, as they exert their real-world control and authority:

> Anna[6]: The idea of a very strong person taking over you. I have this wonderful image of a red cape just . . .
>
> Matilda[7]: It's very seductive, it's almost like taking responsibility away from you.
>
> Anna: Which is entirely different to how I really am.
>
> Matilda: Me too, if someone did try to do that to me I would hate it; it's about seduction really. . . . There are sexual connotations. (Group Interview 2)

As this exchange reveals, there is a central contradiction at the heart of these hyperfeminine performances. On the one hand, women are not expressing attitudes that are in line with traditional constructs of femininity, such as those associated with vulnerability and fragility. In contrast, they are actually using their excessively feminine response to vampire fiction to articulate their strong feminine principles. They use their discussions of these submissive fantasies to communicate their control over their lives in the real world because they would "hate" such behavior to occur in their actual relationships. However, paradoxically, by communicating their desire to relinquish control and allow a "very strong person to take over you," women are also simultaneously reproducing gender roles that reflect what Dunja Brill has termed "the cult of femininity." These performances are essentially "in accord with common cultural norms of femininity" (2008: 42), and serve to reinforce traditional lines of gender.

Women's excessively feminine reading of vampire fiction exposes this central contradiction, but nowhere was this more apparent than during discussions that arose around wearing the corset. As the following section addresses, the vampire community's specific reappropriation of the imitation Victorian whalebone corset as outerwear can be linked to *both* discourses of power, in that it symbolizes women's rejection of thin, slender bodies that have come to dominate popular culture in recent years and also of conformity, as the corset also produces a hyperfeminine shape that allows

Figure 16   Photo shoot of excessive femininity: Demondaz and Hayley Exhayle. Photograph: Angel Lumba—Kingsley Media

Figure 17 Photo shoot of excessive femininity: Demondaz and Hayley Exhayle. Photograph: Jim Nemer

them to reimagine themselves in a time when "women were women," thus once again upholding traditional gender lines and conventional ideas about femininity.

CORSETS

Corsetry remains a constituent of modern fashion in the twenty-first century; whether a corset is worn as a part of a wedding or formal dress, paired with jeans in popular fashion, or in a prized position as a fetish essential, the image of the corset remains prevalent in contemporary culture. However, since the first decade of the twentieth century, the act of *tightlacing*[8] and the everyday wearing of corsetry in mainstream fashion has significantly declined, being replaced by other foundation garments, such as the girdle and brassiere. These items still allowed women to achieve the desired shape but with more comfort, and without the assistance of a maid.

Foundation garments have continued to be popular right up to the present day, as the stays and girdles that women wore in the early part of the twentieth century are now being marketed by popular fashion experts such as Trinny and Susannah and Gok Wan as "power pants," "wonder waspies," and "slicker nickers." Similarly, specialist companies such as What Katie Did and Pandora's Choice also specialize in fifties vintage glamor shapewear, such as bullet bras, girdles, and burlesque lingerie. Therefore, even though the corset may have been phased out of mainstream everyday fashion, it is important to acknowledge its continuation in the twenty-first century, along with the abundance of other foundation undergarments, revealing that women have been shaping their bodies for centuries.

Alongside the current adoption of hidden foundation garments and shapewear to create the illusion of thinness, modern women are also increasingly turning to diet and exercise to sculpt their bodies. Wilson and Ash (1992), Wilson (2003), and Entwistle (2000) assert that in contemporary culture, tensions and restrictions continue to be placed upon the body because bodies are now modified and metaphorically laced from the inside, as the Victorian whalebones have been traded in for gym memberships and healthy eating regimes. Entwistle (2000) cites Wilson and Ash (1992) as she argues that we now have "a modern corset of muscle" in the twenty-first century, and "while the stomach of the nineteenth-century corseted woman was disciplined from the outside, the twentieth century exercising and dieting woman has a stomach disciplined by self discipline" (2000: 20). While this look certainly isn't the only silhouette fashioned in the twenty-first century—for instance, the increasing visibility of voluptuous burlesque stars such as Dita Von Teese and the recent popularity of hourglass style icon Christina Hendricks (star of 1950s-inspired television show *Mad Men*) serve to demonstrate that wider diversity of weights and shapes are available—modern style is indisputably predicated on an obsession with thinness.

In contrast, vampire community members are fashioning a rather different aesthetic to the slender tummies of the contemporary image of beauty. That is not to say they do not possess these attributes but rather that these women find pleasure in celebrating a different type of look. The Edwardian S-bend silhouette is one of the most popular styles adopted by the vampire community. Daniel Delis Hill (2004) explains that at the beginning of the

Edwardian period, the newly redesigned corset introduced a different type of feminine silhouette, which emphasized womanly curves: "The S-Bend silhouette of the Edwardian period represents the last time in fashion history that the mature, full-figured woman was the ideal. The emphasis on ample breasts and rounded hips configured by the S-Bend corset" (2004: 19). In order to achieve this S-bend silhouette, members of the vampire community often wear straight fronted corsets that emphasis their small waistlines. Women also wear padded bodices to achieve full cleavage, and bosoms are pushed tightly together and worn at the front of the outfit (reminiscent of the mono-bosom). Hips are rounded and pushed back by the corset, and some women complete the look with a pad or small bustle in order to accentuate the shape of an S.

As well as reimagining the fashions of the Edwardian period, vampire community members also fashion ideals of beauty that were more generally associated with the Victorian period, and particularly with the Victorian fascination with morbid femininity. As Leigh Summers discusses in *Bound to Please* (2001), Victorian society was a "society that considered female ill health as normative to femininity, and where death and dying leant women a particular if morbid prestige" (2001: 125). Summers notes that tightlacing, the use of white cosmetics containing mercury and lead, the drinking of vinegar, the eating of arsenic,[9] and the painting of blue veins on the neck and brow were some of the more extreme ways that women could increase the effect of a "diaphanous," "soon to leave this world" complexion (2001: 126).[10] This emphasis on pale, white, ethereal skin tones and dark eyes and hair is also rather in keeping with the looks privileged by many members of the vampire community. Women often dye their hair dark brown or black, wear pale foundation, and accentuate eyes and cheekbones with blue and gray makeup in order to achieve a pallid complexion.

Therefore, vampire dress reveals a different type of feminine ideal, as the corset celebrates and accentuates female curves, fashioning an hourglass figure, training the waist, and emphasizing fuller hips and bust. The modern beauty ideal, as demonstrated by the gym tummy, has an altogether different silhouette, accentuating the supple, slender, almost straight-down figure that appears to deemphasize womanly curves. By wearing the corset as outerwear, and constructing an excessively feminine identity, the vampire community is capable of avoiding the modern disciplines of the body. That is not to say that restrictions and confinements do not still press upon and shape their bodies—indeed, the corset is perhaps the most restrictive garment they could select—but by donning this historical vampire identity, women are choosing to fashion an identity outside of their socially sanctioned

Figure 18 Morbid beauty. Photographs: Soulstealer Photography (SoulStealer.co.uk)

roles. This demonstrates once again that through their excessively feminine identity performances (achieved by the corset), women are actually exercising strong feminine ideas as a matter of aberrant choice and agency.

For instance, Rebecca associates the corset precisely with feelings of empowerment and strength. In the following discussion, she likens the experience of being laced into the corset to that of wearing a suit of armor. During this discussion, Rebecca explicitly highlights the paradox of adopting an excessively feminine gender role but simultaneously achieving a strong feminine identity. She identifies the power of the corset as its potential to make the wearer stand out (Williamson 2005) from conventional mainstream dress, due to its historical heritage. She goes on to consider that by sculpting a particular type of body shape, allowing a woman to show off her womanly curves, and by correcting her stance, she is both the object of attention *and* the subject of power. Interestingly, she concludes by commenting on the corset/lacer relationship, stating that when she is laced into her corset she actually feels a sense of power over those who are lacing her, as opposed to experiencing feelings of submission. What is of further interest is that women are now usually laced by their male partner (this is the case for Rebecca) instead of the nineteenth-century servants, maids, and valets (in the case of male corsets), which again reveals an interesting negotiation of male/female gender roles.

> Rebecca: I do feel more ladylike when I wear a corset. I feel very feminine, yet not weak or repressed in any way; quite the opposite in fact. I feel invincible, powerful, strong. Firstly, the corset gives a woman power, as she becomes an object of attention either because wearing a corset is unusual in this day and age, or because she develops womanly curves, which make her both more desirable and enviable. Secondly, the corset is like armor—it feels as though the stiff boning protects you. Wearing the corset makes you stand/sit up straight and makes you more aware of your body and you are more aware of how you are perceived. Standing tall does give you a sense of power and it gives you more grace—you are slimmer, taller. And finally, I have to have somebody to tightlace the corset, which in itself gives you a sense of power, or gives the illusion of having someone at your beck and call to fasten the corset. (Group Interview 1)

Similarly, historical costume maker and custom-made corsetière Madame le Strange notes that the revisiting of the historical corset does not begin and end with the vampire community but is also notable across wider subcultural communities. For example, Madame le Strange discusses how she creates designs for a range of different styles including retro, fifties pinup, burlesque, and fetish, as well as Victorian, Edwardian, Elizabethan, and medieval styles. She suggests that women's return to the corset is associated with power and in taking pride in dressing differently, celebrating real women and enjoying the voluptuous female form:

> I absolutely loathe the fact that the majority of people appear to just copy verbatim what they see in magazines, catalogs, and shop windows, or on pop stars or people on the television. I also despise that in order to achieve this somewhat despotic "ideal" people are starving themselves, or becoming hooked on the adrenaline surges they get from working out. . . . And what's wrong with having curves? I'm not using that as a euphemism for being overweight, I'm saying that women are supposed to have curves. What is wrong with embracing one's femininity, or even

enhancing it? . . . Why are women returning to corseting? I think one might as well ask why we wish to feel attractive. I feel the two go hand in hand. And I also think that we've finally realized we can be empowered and still be feminine. We don't have to be the aggressive power-suit wearing executive of the '80s, we don't have to cut our hair short, don army fatigues, and protest on Greenham Common, and we certainly don't have to burn our bras. We can be what we are . . . beautiful, intelligent women, capable of holding down a career and raising a family, and we can look good while we're at it! (Madame le Strange)

Madame le Strange presents a compelling argument concerning the empowering potentials of the corset and reveals that some women (herself and Rebecca included) may be consciously using their body to explore subversive ideas. However, at this stage it is important to avoid getting swept away with the defiant possibilities of vampire identity and refrain from viewing every woman in a corset as an organized act of feminist "social rebellion" (Spooner 2000: 196). It is more accurate to acknowledge that although there are women who select feminine dress practices in order to construct identity on their own (politicized) terms, it is much more common for women to be less attached to conscious ideologies of power and more concerned with taste and aesthetics. For these women, the selection of the corset is often tied up with size and shapism issues, and the fact that more conventional fashion styles do not accommodate fuller figures.

Although these women may not be articulating fully fledged feminist principles, in smaller, more muted ways they use excessively feminine identity performances to make a positive difference to their daily lives, as the following exchange between Lou and Rebecca reveals:

Rebecca: Wearing the corset, it's very feminine.
Lou: The whole kind of Victorian and gothic look lends itself to the fuller, curvy figure. At least you can be proud of your assets! The tiny waist, the voluptuous figure, it's almost like the ultimate feminine image. (Group Interview 1)

So although it must be borne in mind that these women are still essentially forced to remain outside of the sanctioned gender system and reside within marginal groups that are more often than not positioned as "Other" in society, and are often "dealt pain and injuries" (McRobbie 2005: 87) due to their subcultural appearance (whether in the form of small-scale ridicule, in response to their perceivably alienating femininity, as documented during the Victorian pub crawl in chapter 3, or more serious cases of actual bodily harm, as described by MorbidFrog in chapter 2), wearing corsets and a feminine style of dress does have its rewards. The excessive femininity discourse reveals that vampire style affords women self-confidence, choice, and feelings of independence—a positive move in the right direction.

ANDROGYNY AND VARIATION

Thus far, the excessive femininity discourse is in line with what Dunja Brill has termed the "cult of femininity," as like the goth women of Brill's study who prize styles that are "far more in accord with common cultural norms of femininity" (2008: 42), vampire community members also predominantly reveal hyperfeminine modes of dress, which serve to reaffirm and consolidate conventional femininity (although, as we have seen, this does not necessarily entirely close down possibilities for empowerment). As Brill goes on to illustrate during her discussion of Petit Scarabee, in the "Claiming Androgyny" section of *Goth Culture* (2008), although the "cult of femininity" is far more popular with goths, in rare instances female androgyny has also been fashioned on the goth scene. For Brill, these androgynous displays serve an empowering function because they offer women a "source of rebellion and strength" both inside and outside the subculture (2008: 72). However, female androgyny also simultaneously compromises women's subcultural capital, as more masculine looks are not generally privileged among goths:

> Through distancing herself from women inside and outside the subculture who in her view embody a derivative and vacant image of femininity, Petit Scarabee claims female androgyny as a source of rebellion and strength for herself. In doing so, she implicitly lays claim to the masculinist tradition of rebellious androgyny, which is normally reserved to males in the Gothic scene. On the subjective level, androgyny thus has an important empowering function for her; however, it should be noted that there are no subcultural rewards or recognition for such acts of gender-bending. As I have shown before, Goth women's style is judged mainly by aesthetic criteria and the cultural relevance of female gender play is not acknowledged. Consequently an androgynous style does nothing to boost a woman's subcultural capital. (Brill 2008: 72)

Similar cases of gender-bending were also evident within the vampire community, but in contrast to Brill's research, androgynous and unisex styles are comparatively more positively received because female gender play *is* increasingly acknowledged within vampire subculture. The increased rewards and recognition for androgynous styles within the vampire community are due to two predominant factors. First, unlike the goth scene, the vampire community's close attachment to the vampire legend has led to a level of inspiration or costuming of vampire media. Although women do adorn themselves in the style of female characters such as Sookie (*True Blood*), Drusilla (*Buffy the Vampire Slayer*), and Queen Akasha (*Queen of the Damned*), the abundance of male vampire characters within popular culture has (in rare cases) led to the adoption of more masculine styles of dress. For example, by her own admission, Jenny's white, cropped haircut is styled in homage to David (Kiefer Sutherland) from *The Lost Boys*.

Second, and with far greater impact, the increased acknowledgement of androgyny among vampire style is also linked to important developments that have taken place since Brill's publication in 2008, as steampunk style has diffused across vampire and wider subcultural communities. Although the vast majority of steampunk outfits worn by women are in line with the historical beauty aesthetic (outfits often include corsetry, bustles, full skirts, pantaloons, and waisted frock coats that accentuate the waist, bust, and hips), women have also indicated that steampunk androgyny and cross-dressing can be extremely pleasurable. For example, Audrey, the alternative jewelry maker and model, communicates that she usually dresses in more feminine styles, being influenced by neo-Victoria and elegant gothic Lolita, but engages in a specifically androgynous style of dress for steampunk events:

> Audrey: For me, steampunk represents freedom. I don't feel like I am trapped into that goth/vampire look, wearing only black. I really don't want to get stuck into one category. I can invent myself in a whole new world and I can make my own style. . . . For example, I think it's really good for women to dress in a unisex style. I love to wear the little three-quarter length trousers and high-necked blouses, hair in a ponytail and no cleavage. I feel really good like that. I think with steampunk you can adapt it to suit yourself. (Individual Interview 5)

Many members of the vampire community, who have thus far performed hyperfeminine identities, are increasingly using steampunk to play out contradictory performances. This has been a marked development from the early steampunk styles fashioned by the community at events such as Vampyre Villains versus Steampunk Slayers Costume Showdown Part I, which were comparatively more feminine. More recently, outfits fashioned at Vampyre Villains versus Steampunk Slayers Part II and Lincoln's Weekend at the Asylum steampunk festival reveal a far more sophisticated and androgynous approach. Women have commented on how they dress in deliberately inauthentic clothing that allows a full range of movement. This is exemplified in the Girl

Genius archetype (from the comic of the same name) that signifies an active femininity. Although this look may include a corset, it also involves pairing pantaloons and shorter skirts with goggles and tools, to suggest the female steampunk is taking on the traditional male role of inventor or steamship mechanic. Similarly, waistcoats, long sleeve shirts, and garments such as spats in materials such as tweed and corduroy create an androgynous appearance. Therefore, going back to the research questions posed at the end of chapter 3, this discourse reveals that although the majority of women may be dressing themselves in excessively feminine ways, there are also variations of vampire performance occurring. Although much rarer, women can also select from

Figure 19 Steampunk development, from femininity to androgyny. Photographs: Soulstealer Photography (SoulStealer.co.uk)

more androgynous and unisex styles, which allows them freedom from being trapped into one specific type of vampire look, demonstrating that there are exceptions to the cult of femininity rule.

Similar to discourses of androgyny, discourses about race also reveal a degree of variation in women's experiences. Although in general discourses concerning race were not common throughout this research, it is important to keep in mind that the morbid beauty aesthetic, which includes a gothic diaphanous look of dark hair and pale white skin is certainly not privileged by all members of the community. Although the vampire community is a predominantly white, middle-class culture and is generally positioned in opposition to more urban style cultures (such as hip hop and rap culture), the community also contains people from wider racial and ethnic groups who do not privilege the diaphanous aesthetic to the same degree.

For example, Ronita[11] is mixed race and explains how the rarity of her complexion in the community is actually a point of curiosity for people inside and outside the subculture, and she has always met an extremely positive response because of her difference. More specifically, as the following discussion reveals, Ronita feels that she may receive more positive treatment from outsiders and what she terms the "hoodie" or "chav"[12] culture due to her mixed-race appearance. In fact, she suggests that such groups may have displayed more antisocial behavior towards her if she were white:

> Ronita: Because I am mixed race, it creates a bit more of a curiosity, the "chavs" around here, the way they act—the kind of gangster thing, they are curious. If I was a goth and not mixed race I think I would get more insults. Goths are known to be white, but they make their skin even whiter, and they are famous for their dyed black hair, pale white skin, that is the ideal goth look. . . . But obviously, as a mixed-race goth I can't really do that, so as a result there is more of a curiosity. I was in a pub in East London once, and a couple called me over and said, "I hope you don't get offended by our staring, but our son is goth, and after meeting all of his friends we have never seen a mixed-race goth." (Individual Interview 1)

Ronita's discussion about race reveals that there are pleasures to be had in standing out (Williamson 2005) from both conventional and alternative style. Ronita not only stands out from more conventional style due to her gothic appearance but also stands out from the community,[13] as she does not sport the ideal gothic look of a pale white complexion. Therefore, through the discourse of androgyny and variation, it is possible to view a full spectrum of vampire identities that, although they are more rarely performed, demonstrate wider attractions than excessive femininity and morbid beauty.

IDENTIFICATION AND OUTSIDERDOM

The discourses of the romanticization of the past, excessive femininity, and androgyny and variation all reveal the fluid, and at times contradictory, experiences of the female members of the vampire community. Women sign up to the community for different reasons. For some women, community membership is an aesthetic decision, as fashioning vampiric styles of dress is actually associated with a love for the historical, which allows them to dwell in neo-Victorian architectures where they reimagine the past in real-world contexts. For others, such dress practices are also tied up with size and shapism issues, as corsets and bustled skirts flatter the fuller, voluptuous figure and vampire dress permits women to feel feminine in a way that conventional femininity does not. Alternatively, community membership also provides women with opportunities to enjoy more androgynous styles of dress, which makes them stand out from both conventional society and the community as a whole, giving them freedom from being trapped into one singular type of subcultural image.

The final discourse this chapter will now address is concerned with women's identification with the figure of the vampire, and discourses of isolation, as for other women vampire community membership provides a cathartic function, allowing them to draw on vampire media to make sense of their own feelings of isolation and pain in response to not fitting in to more normative, mainstream aspects of society. This is in keeping with Milly Williamson's (2005) findings, as Williamson suggests that the female vampire fans of her study may identify with the plight of onscreen vampires because they feel similar experiences of alienation and "the pathos of being locked in circumstances beyond one's control, forced to be an outsider" (2005: 145).

This discussion will once again return to women's experiences of the vampire in childhood, as many women identify this as the period their identification with the vampire and wider horror fiction began. During their childhood years, respondents discussed how they consumed gothic fiction, poetry, and novels, from the *Little Vampire* books to the fiction of Bram Stoker and Dennis Wheatley. Many women also discussed interests in horror, including both real-life horror stories from books about Jewish concentration camps (discussed by Anna, during Group Interview 2), to more veiled horror stories, such as *Grimm's Fairy Tales*, that had not been cleaned up by the Disney adaptations (discussed by Beth, during Individual Interview 4). One participant noted how she was drawing blood-spattered princesses from as young as four years of age (VC18, Questionnaire). Fans expressed a number of different reasons for their consumption of gothic and horror literature in childhood, but the two predominant themes that emerged were associated with reading vampire fiction as a historical romance (as discussed previously) and, more importantly for this discussion, identification with the Other (and particularly the isolation of the vampire).

Brigid Cherry's (2002) work on female audiences of horror films can be most useful in understanding this relationship between childhood pleasures in the gothic and adult preoccupations with horror/vampirism. Cherry identifies various female attractions in the horror film, including the strong female lead, high production values, historical costume design, and reading horror from a romance perspective. Similar to the vampire community, Cherry discusses that many female horror fans also consumed images of horror before adolescence. She states that "several reported that their first experience of horror involved being enjoyably frightened by Disney animated films and other dark children's films based on fairy tales" (2002: 173). Cherry suggests that part of the fascination with horror (and particularly the vampire film) in adult life goes back to childhood identification and fascination with the monster. Similar to children's fictions, such as the fairy tale, "horror films share the frequent representation of distortions of natural forms—supernatural monsters with a human face, for instance" (2002: 173).

As Cherry outlines, it is these images of monstrosity that women found themselves identifying with, as they saw cathartic parallels with their own feelings of outsiderdom as children, and later as adults. During this study, a number of women discussed identifying variously with the vampire from a very young age. However, this identification with images of onscreen isolation was particularly evident with one female respondent called Beth,[14] who suffers from a neurological condition that has affected her ability to form close social relationships, and consequently she finds it difficult to cope with social situations. Beth felt that because of her disability, she has always found herself on the outside of society, and thus identified with images of isolation in vampire cinema from a young age. More recently, she discusses how this sense of isolation has led to her identification with the character of Drusilla from *Buffy the Vampire Slayer*:

Beth: I found Drusilla absolutely fascinating. It wasn't just her dress sense; I thought her character was just so interesting. Angel, the vampire that turned her just left her all alone. I identify with Drusilla because she was in the position where she was in a mentally vulnerable state; no one gave a damn, everyone left her, everyone around her was just contributing to her mental state. I just felt so sorry and sad for her. . . . I think it is better sometimes to shut yourself off from people, because if you can't mix with them, they just torment you. (Individual Interview 4)

It is also this sense of empathy and identification with onscreen vampires that has inspired her own dress practices, as she fashions aspects of the show as part of her alternative everyday lifestyle. With regard to dressing her body, Beth discusses how she may imitate and make her own clothes to look like vampire figures that she identifies with. Beth goes on to suggest that she is particularly influenced by the Lolita-style clothes worn by Drusilla and other examples of female vampire film characters, such as Mina in *Bram Stoker's Dracula*. She discusses how her fascination with Lolita fashion also stems from her interest in Japanese culture and her perception that the customs are more amenable to her lifestyle.

> Beth: I like Drusilla as she wears the Lolita style of clothing, the big frills; because of her mental state they dress her like she is a little girl. I tend to use Lolita-style blouses, big lace bonnets. It's a case of mixing periods; it's very Victorian. I have studied Japanese culture; it's interesting, the idea that a society is so rigid in rules and customs it's difficult to put a foot wrong. But in this society, if you don't have the ability to know what's acceptable it's difficult, if you don't know how a situation works, you have to watch it. That's what I have had to do since I was a little girl. (Individual Interview 4)

For Beth, onscreen vampires appear to serve a cathartic function because she can align her experiences, and specifically the anxieties she feels in social situations, with the character of Drusilla, allowing her to cope and deal with difficult issues. As Beth continued to talk about various other examples of vampire cinema, she discussed her responses in a highly visceral manner, revealing an extremely in-depth engagement with the fictional world of the narrative and an almost sensory identification with the vampire character, and specifically with the pain they experience. For example, when talking about the film *Blade*, and the vampire's need for blood, she provides an extremely detailed response to the pain that the vampire suffers:

> Beth: Blood is the source of life, and it makes sense vampires need it. *Blade* is cheesy, but they covered a very interesting point, as on a very metaphysical level they explore how it could be possible to need to drink blood. Because vampires have a very low red blood cell count, so they need human blood to stop their immune system from crashing. If they don't get it, the red blood cells shrivel up; if you can imagine every cell in your body drying up, the end of your nerve cells would be screaming and that would send them mad. It would feel like stinging nettles on the inside. You know when you sleep and get your arm trapped and it goes all tingly, it would be worse than that on the inside. I can't imagine anything more painful. (Individual Interview 4)

This complex and extremely invested physical response to pain in the film's narrative reveals Beth's own displaced emotional pain. This is in keeping with Williamson's (2005) and Bacon-Smith's (1992, 2000) studies of female fans of vampires and of science fiction. Although Williamson is discussing the process of writing vampire fan fiction, she notes how the vampire can be used as a "transformation story" to allow fans a fantasy transcendence (2005: 165). Drawing on the work of Bacon-Smith, Williamson states that vampire fans often "talk story," elaborating on interesting themes of the narrative, plot, and characters while simultaneously discussing their own disguised pain (2005: 168). She suggest that "[t]he vampire transformation story, however, emphasises physical pain and the mental anguish it generates, rather than psychic pain" (2005: 168). Therefore, as this example illustrates, Beth's identification with onscreen vampires serves a soothing function, as she is able to use the fantasy diegesis to explore and understand aspects of her own predicament in place of the close social relationships that she finds difficult to form. Through vampire culture, women demonstrate their identification both performatively, through dressing like celluloid vampires, and through cathartic processes of transformation and talking.

Therefore, having established the underlying discourses that have emerged from the vampire community, it is increasingly evident that the motivations behind vampire community allegiance are varied. These range from acting out hyperfeminine performances that center on romantic, historical themes to wider scenarios of gender play and androgyny. As well as creating opportunities for these heavily gendered performances, responses from Beth and Audrey also demonstrate that vampire culture is associated with cathartic pleasures, as women draw on vampire and gothic imagery to reimagine identities that are more appealing to them, dreaming alternative scenarios of class and luxury (in the case of Audrey and steampunk) and thrashing out anxieties of isolation and exclusion (in the case of Beth and vampire media) to make a difference in their daily lives. Needless to say, the attractions of vampire culture are plentiful and offer very different things to different women.

However, how women's difference from each other plays out within the vampire community remains unresolved, as these different experiences can often lead to antagonistic relationships and pecking orders. As Sarah Thornton's research of subcultural capital so usefully highlights, there are different currencies of subcultural capital operating within the community, and women can be positioned as high and low, or rich and poor in vampire status, which consequently impacts on their overall experience of community life. The next chapter will investigate the community dimension of the vampire subculture in more detail and take a closer look at *both* high-profile members, whose abundance of subcultural capital affords them a disproportionate amount of respect and notoriety within the group, and those members who exist on the outskirts, who at times feel excluded and shut out. If there are subcultural standards of behavior and codes of appropriate dress that facilitate entry into the vampire community (as the *Chronicles* article "Are We R.O.A.Ring Loud Enough" suggests), then what is in store for those who do not want to or who simply cannot conform to the vampire front?

−6−

Alternative Celebrity

As was discussed in the previous chapter, the vampire community's dress and aesthetics reveal varied and contrasting experiences of femininity. Although dress practices are extremely eclectic, and identities are fluid and variable, on the whole, the vampire community selects from a wide palette of vampire aesthetics and presents a *group* vampire identity, revealing a similar level of homology to those subcultures discussed by Dick Hebdige. By using the example of punks, Hebdige explains subcultures' paradoxical relationship to cultural objects, stating that punks were "clothed in chaos," but only managed to convey such chaos through an ordered style of signifying practice (1979: 114), demonstrating that there is an inherent conformity within alternative subcultures. Members of the vampire community also fashion diverse cult objects of fandom that include fangs, parasols, dyed black hair, dark makeup, pale complexions, the wearing of black, veils, body art (depicting bats, skulls, fairies etc), piercings, corsets, bustled skirts, and a whole host of Victorian, Edwardian, and steampunk ensembles.

The appropriation of these objects maintains the boundaries of the subculture, as members are presenting or conforming to a vampire front (Goffman 1959). This then allows members to demonstrate their individuality and resistance to conventional style (and separate themselves from outsiders), but it also allows them to seek out a community of likeminded others (i.e., people within the subculture). This is also in keeping with Hodkinson's research in *Goth*, which highlights how members of the goth subculture reveal a central focus on both individuality and commitment to the community (2002: 76). In his chapter "Insiders and Outsiders," Hodkinson states that "whether in terms of intensity or longevity of individual participation, depth of knowledge and understanding, or even involvement in production and organisation of activities, goths tended to regard themselves as strongly committed" (2002: 78).

This relationship between individuality and conformity, and insiders and outsiders, is rather complex when considering the vampire community because unlike the punk, skinhead, or even goth communities, what separates the vampire community from being a purely subcultural grouping is the fact that the community also exists as a fan culture.[1] Therefore, this insider/outsider status is immediately problematized because the community is made up of a range of different people, including those who would class themselves as alternative as well as members who dress in entirely conventional styles outside of community events. Thus, while the majority of members may desire to fashion their subcultural status in a similar way to that of youth or music cultures, such as engaging in a vampire lifestyle and revealing their interest in the historical vampire on their bodies, there are varying levels of participation occurring, and not all members are gravitating around performance and presenting cult objects to the same degree (for instance, as chapter 4 illustrates, there is a very small proportion of the community who do not consider their dress to be alternative or vampire-inspired at all).

Needless to say, the hybrid nature of the vampire community, with its extremely diverse range of positions, can often lead to antagonistic results. For instance, during early stages of participant observation, I quickly noticed that vampire community events were organized around specific cliques and selective groupings. As I continued to attend meetings at the London Vampyre Group, the Vampyre Connexion, and the London Vampire Meetup Group, I noted that night after night, similar people would cluster in similar areas of the respective venues. These mini-groupings also continued online; the wall posting, photographs, and diary entries on people's online social media networks continued to reveal the clusters of friendship groups. As I began to talk to women in more detail during the individual and group interview stage, I was able to ask specific questions about the dynamics of the community and how it was organized. This exposed notable inconsistencies in members' experiences of the community, and more specifically the different ways that people are positioned across the subculture. It soon became apparent that there are two opposing ends of the vampire community spectrum. At one end there are high-profile celebrity members, who fashion the most elaborated vampire identities and experience more prestigious positions within the community. At the other, there were those who feel excluded from the wider community, who struggle to make friends and gain acceptance into the group. For some of these members, dress is a peer pressure–induced obligation, as opposed to being a genuine expression of their interests in alternative culture and the vampire.

Therefore, this chapter will begin by addressing how the vampire community might be organized around high-profile members who possess high levels of subcultural capital and can be considered style leaders. Although the work of Sarah Thornton (1995) has been particularly useful when attempting to understand subcultural positions and status and how one can be in or out, high or low in subcultural capital, more recent work by Matt Hills on celebrity fans will be drawn upon in detail throughout this discussion. In his chapter "Not Just Another Powerless Elite? When Media Fans become Subcultural Celebrities," Hills (2006) develops and expands theories of subcultural capital and presents a model of how fans are able to raise their status to that of subcultural celebrity. According to Hills, "celebrity and fandom may not, after all, constitute entirely reified and separate concepts/experiences" (2006: 101–2).

Through case study analysis of the Vampyre Connexion social secretary, MorbidFrog—a particularly well-known member of the community who was continually referenced during interviews—this research will provide an account of how community members' ordinary description of online and offline subcultural capital (from writing blogs and diary entries to posting photography) transforms them into an "extraordinary" person or "hybridized fan-celebrity," with a disproportionate, nonreciprocal position in the subculture (2006: 103). The discussion will establish MorbidFrog's reach as a fan, style leader, and social network user and the celebrity properties that she possesses. Once the discussion has illustrated how the community is organized in terms of subcultural celebrity and the impacts this has on other members' positions, this chapter will also consider whether some members of the community exist outside of the community front and do not gravitate around subcultural celebrity, as interviews revealed that members frequently recognized the cliques and selective nature of their own community.

SUBCULTURAL CELEBRITY

The definition of *celebrity* is increasingly difficult to pin down. In *Understanding Celebrity*, Graeme Turner suggests that concepts of celebrity are highly varied and contingent, linked with recognition and disproportionate interest from the public sphere (2004: 3). Sean Redmond, in his chapter "Intimate Fame Everywhere," suggests that fame is a ubiquitous cultural phenomenon that has the potential to offer heightened levels of intimacy for ordinary and extraordinary people (2006: 29). He suggests that new media technologies, such as social networking sites, appear to be altering the definitions of fame, and the experiences of fan/celebrity boundaries, at ever-increasing rates. New media therefore reveals how people may be transformed into the extraordinary through engagement with the most ordinary aspects of the everyday.

In line with Redmond's discussion of celebrity and the impacts of new media, boyd and Ellison (2007) also discuss how changes in the way we use the Internet have contributed to heightened levels of personal intimacy that has been termed the egocentric shift. They note a shift in focus from interests and topical discussions, as demonstrated by earlier forums, e-mail, and Usenet groups, to more individual or egocentric perspectives that are exemplified by social network sites, such as Facebook and Twitter, which are more person-centric than group-centric. As Mark Deuze notes, this has increased the potential for people to become *"egocasters"* (Rosen 2004, in Deuze 2005) that live in a thoroughly individualized culture that is dominated by personal technologies, as consuming has become synonymous with producing.

This shift has contributed to the celebrification of members of fan communities and subcultures, as it has opened up cultural space in which a new type of celebrity can perform. Members of the vampire community who have the desire, time, and ability to use these sites, as well as engaging in other offline subcultural activities, may experience processes of celebrification, or as Hills (2006) suggests, they might become subcultural celebrities. Hills draws on Andrea MacDonald's (1998) research of science fiction fandoms when considering a potential research model for subcultural celebrity, as he suggests that "the range of interlocking hierarchies identified by MacDonald (1998) can thus be argued to underpin fans' subcultural celebrity" (2006: 105). MacDonald presents five hierarchies that are integral to achieving subcultural celebrity status, including *knowledge, access, leaders, fandom level,* and *venue.*[2] Of these categories, fans may rank highly in one or two or, alternatively, like MorbidFrog, may have a high status across all five.

While these hierarchies are extremely useful when attempting to establish examples of subcultural celebrity within the vampire community, as Hills suggests, there also needs to be a further discussion of the role of subcultural/niche mediation, as it is also possible to achieve celebrity through more specific areas of subcultural production, such as those concerned with style and commodification. Therefore, the following case study adapts MacDonald's hierarchies to include a sixth category, which I have titled *hierarchy of performance*, in an attempt to account for how the commodification of vampire culture affects a member's position within the community.

CASE STUDY OF MORBIDFROG

Knowledge

According to MacDonald (1998), the first hierarchy to consider is the hierarchy of knowledge. This is concerned with how a fan's position within a specific community is determined by the knowledge he or she holds of the fictional universe. When applying this principle to MorbidFrog, there are two potential acquisitions of knowledge to consider that link directly to the nature of the community as both a fan culture and identity subculture. They consist of either the knowledge associated with fan object (i.e., vampire films, television, and literature) or the knowledge associated with the subculture/community practices (i.e., the subcultural capital associated with events and with lifestyle activities). First, when considering the level of fan knowledge MorbidFrog possesses with regard to the fictional world, or fan object (i.e., the vampire), it is apparent that she appears to hold specialist knowledge of such vampire/occult mythology and media.

During in-depth interviews, MorbidFrog discussed how she consumes a great deal of vampire media. This includes books such as Bram Stoker's *Dracula*, Anne Rice's *Vampire Chronicles*, Richard Matheson's *I Am Legend,* Merlin Coverley's *Occult London*, television series including *Ultraviolet*, and films as diverse as Klaus Kinski's performance in *Phantom der Nacht* as well as *Brotherhood of the Wolf*, *The Hunger*, and Hammer Horror. Her Facebook profile also includes the finer details of the books she is currently reading and some reviews of such media. However, despite the fact that MorbidFrog is an aficionado of the vampire, and demonstrates her interest in the genre on her profile pages, by her own admission, she does not post profusely on the subject.

> MorbidFrog: We don't talk about vampire films or books that often; if a book or film comes out, like the book *The Historian*, that created some online discussion, and if I see a film extremely worth mentioning, then I might document it. So it will come up sometimes, I suppose, but I wouldn't set up a specific discussion; it's just part of our everyday life. The same with my fangs. I wear them every time I go out; like my corset, it's part of the everyday. (Individual Interview 3)

MorbidFrog appears to view vampire films, books, and mythology as she does her dress practices: ingrained into her everyday life. Therefore, unlike some other fan groups that may have hierarchies of diegetic knowledge (e.g., *Star Trek* and *Dr. Who*), with some fans possessing extremely detailed information, and in some instances even competing over knowledge (see Hills 2002: 46), this kind of knowledge capital is not necessarily highly prized by the women of the vampire community. This may be partly because knowledge acquisition is actually more often associated with masculine fan responses, as Joanne Hollows (2003) identifies during her discussion of cult collectors. Hollows notes that in the past cult fans have been constructed as masculine "collectors" and "manly adventurers" (2003: 47), and although research suggests that both men and women engage in collecting practices, women's collections contain more personal and intimate objects while men prize rarity, authenticity, and acquiring collectibles before their friends (Tashiro 1996, in Hollows 2003: 47).

Therefore, if high-profile members such as MorbidFrog are not concerned with this type of knowledge acquisition, and many of their conversations at face-to-face events, forum postings, blogs, and diary entries are rather far removed from vampire topics and discussions, what equates to desirable knowledge? As chapter 4 shows, the answer to this question is tied up with the subcultural nature of the community. For many of the more performative members of the community, such as MorbidFrog, knowledge of the subculture (dress, activities, and events) rather than the vampire itself is the currency of the vampire community.

For instance, going back to Hollow's account of gendered collectors and the tendency for women to collect more personal and intimate objects, MorbidFrog appears to bear out this thesis, as her Facebook page catalogs her in-depth knowledge of subcultural dress and her own personal creativity. In the Facebook notes section, she uploads photography and writes diary entries that document her subcultural creations. Popular threads include Attempting Elizabethan Hair and Makeup (2011), which contains photographs of MorbidFrog recreating complex Elizabethan hairstyles, comprising plaits, extensions, and hair jewelry (see Figure 20) as well as the Birdcage on My Head (2010) thread, which documents the various stages of her latest millinery construction—a purple and green vintage birdcage hat, complete with imitation bird, stemmed roses, and foliage. Similarly, under the My First Cushions subject line, she has uploaded images from her sewing class, documenting various cushions she has made from old T-shirts associated with the subculture. She states, "Great sewing class last night. I learned how to make cushions using some of my too small T-shirts, . . . so I now have Inkkies [Inkubus Sukkubus] and Theatres des Vampires cushions" (MorbidFrog Facebook notes, 2011). Once they have viewed these images, friends can then post words of praise and encouragement, revealing their interest and appetite for MorbidFrog's creativity. Specific comments include, "Great way to

Figure 20 MorbidFrog Elizabethan makeup and hairstyle. Photograph: Soulstealer Photography (SoulStealer.co.uk)

re-use old T-shirts. Really inspired" and "This is fab, we look forward to seeing your final outfit and hair doo. Love seeing your pics on here, your outfits
are fab, well done you!"

As well as her in-depth knowledge of dress and accessories, MorbidFrog
also has unrivalled knowledge of subcultural activities. First, her time-rich
lifestyle facilitates her knowledge of the subculture, as she is able to engage
in an array of subcultural activities on a daily basis, from elaborate everyday
dress practices to a high level of participation online or offline, without too many
external constraints. For instance, during the period of research, MorbidFrog

was a single female with no children, living away from her family in France. Her occupation as a London university librarian allows her to spend the majority of her day online and also places few restrictions on her dress code. Second, MorbidFrog also takes up official responsibilities within the community, fulfilling the role of Vampyre Connexion social secretary and online events publicist. These positions provide her with a unique insight into the inner workings of the vampire community, as she organizes and attends most of the meetings, parties, and community outings. Therefore her in-depth knowledge of vampire media, subcultural dress, and lifestyle activities reveal her richness in this category and are contributing factors in her celebrification.

Access and Fandom Level

MacDonald describes the hierarchy of access as concerned with fans that have access to the show's (i.e., fan object's) actors, producers, personnel, and, in some rare cases, the actual shooting of the show (MacDonald 1998, in Hills 2006). However, unlike fans of *Dr. Who* or *Stargate*, the vampire community members enjoy a variety of vampire and horror media rather than being attached to one particular text, and they are actually rather removed from the fan object. Therefore, rather than focusing on MorbidFrog's access to vampire media production, what is more important to consider is her access to the subculture as a whole.[3]

MorbidFrog has adopted a gatekeeping position at the Vampyre Connexion, fulfilling the role of new members' representative. In this sense, MorbidFrog not only holds extensive knowledge of the subculture but also provides access to the community, both online and face-to-face, for new members. She introduces them to other participants, providing them with the information they require and also following up on their experiences after meetings. For example, when conducting research into the community, MorbidFrog initially aided my own access to the vampire community. Upon my first visit to the Vampyre Connexion on January 25, 2007, held at the Blue Posts, Soho, I was initially greeted by the Vampyre Master Colin and his wife Jenny. I was then immediately introduced to MorbidFrog, who spent a large proportion of the evening introducing me to other members and explaining the relative histories of the community, thereby fulfilling a gatekeeping role and providing me with an entry point into the subculture. As I discovered during the evening, MorbidFrog's access to the community far exceeds the Vampyre Connexion, as she attends and publicizes numerous activities across all three vampire communities and wider subcultural events. She describes her position as follows:

MorbidFrog: I am the event organizer, the promoter. I deal with everything to do with parties, because I am aware of what's going on in London, especially on the alternative scene, and particularly the goth-related events. I like to keep people informed so people have a choice. I am also members' rep, so I make sure that if anyone new comes to the meeting I chat to them, introduce them, and then follow up later. It wasn't planned for me to be the online face, but because I am online a lot, I do most of the online promotions. But I also promote other things; this weekend I was a promoter for gigs. When I was on the table selling T-shirts I did a little plug for the Vampyre Connexion. (Individual Interview 3)

Similarly, the hierarchy of fandom level continues to reveal MorbidFrog's high subcultural capital. This hierarchy is concerned with subcultural participation; those who attend organized fan events versus those who do not. From the About Me section on her MySpace profile and on her Facebook wall, it is evident that MorbidFrog participates in various subcultural activities, such as attending various goth clubs, bars, and meetups, including Vampyre Connexion meetings, Vampire Meetup, The Dev, Bibliogoth, Kryptorium, Not Malice, Dead and Buried, Invocation, Black Mass, Fright Club, Wave-Gotik-Treffen (Leipzig Festival), and Whitby Goth Weekend. During interviews she discussed her normal weekend activities.

MorbidFrog: I went to Tanz Macabre last night, a really nice tiny little club in the basement of a goth club. It's dark and lots of the people from the community go there; it has fantastic music. I went to Slimelight on Saturday that's been going for over twenty years. And Friday I was at Inferno at the Electric Ballroom. Sometimes I go to metal clubs, sometimes burlesque; that's the thing in London, everything is there for you and you can pick and choose as you wish. (Individual Interview 3)

As well as her involvement with club promotions and the music scene, MorbidFrog is also extremely interested in various other cultural activities. Like the majority of the community, she is middle class and well educated. She holds a degree in visual arts and ceramics and a postgraduate master's degree in library and information studies. She hosts talks at Treadwells bookshop, and writes for the Vampyre Connexion fanzine, *Dark Nights*. She describes other activities associated with high culture, such as art exhibitions, museums, and how she has found many likeminded people in the subculture:

MorbidFrog: It was at the Vampyre Connexion that I found people with the same tastes as me, interested in the artistic side. Yes I love goth music and dancing, but I love art, I love theatre, I love it when I meet people standing

> outside a loud club and we are able to talk about the latest pre-Raphaelite exhibition, or go and visit a gothic church somewhere. It was fantastic to meet a group of people who love to dress up, love to visit places, and who love the same movies; there is always something going on. (Individual Interview 3)

Such immersion in vampire culture and participation in events associated with clubbing, rock music, alternative dress, and a general expression of individuality and difference as demonstrated by MorbidFrog, are aspects that are often associated with youth culture. J. P. Telotte (1991) suggests the activities of cult fans are often associated with youth subcultures and suggests that both age and social situation are impacting factors on these groups. The middle-class teenager and young adult may attempt to exist outside of the cultural mainstream as a kind of "rite of passage" (1991: 10). Similarly, Hollows (2003) states that subcultures are

> actively produced by young people themselves: defined by their distance from commerce; and more "authentic"; [they] are a means for young people to express their difference; and are, therefore, deviant, resistant or transgressive. (2003: 36)

As MorbidFrog's high fandom level demonstrates, MorbidFrog is essentially continuing to fashion a youthful identity into her thirties (she is thirty-four). The extension of youth in modern culture has meant that such youth cultures can no longer be restricted to the 18–24 age bracket. MorbidFrog is still engaging in many practices associated with youth culture and may continue to do so for many years to come.

Therefore, as MorbidFrog's experiences reveal, it is evident once again that the pleasures of being a member of the vampire community are increasingly tied to group subcultural participation, and activities often associated with youth/music cultures. Although MorbidFrog is rich in knowledge of the vampire as well as the subculture, through her own admission, her subcultural involvement does outweigh her vampire fan involvement, in keeping with the wider experiences of other members. For example, other participants, such as Lou, demonstrate the privileging of knowledge capital associated with the community and social activities over fan interest in the vampire. Lou reveals a limited investment in the cultural pursuits relating to the figure of the vampire, noting that "I have brought the *Dracula* novel, but what kind of fan am I if I have not even read it? . . . The community for me is for general socializing. I have made so many friends" (Group Interview 3).

Leaders

MorbidFrog's celebrification is therefore partly due to her knowledge, dedicated fandom level, and unique access to the subculture. Established members of the vampire community who share a strong interest in these subcultural activities can rely on MorbidFrog to provide information about future events, while new members can use her as a gatekeeper, or guide to the subculture. Therefore, many community members do organize around subcultural celebrity because such high-profile members make the interests of the group more transparent, as they articulate (albeit it in a much more elaborated and verifiable way) the wider pleasures of the grouping, including attending events, talking online, demonstrating individuality and difference, and being part of a wider community.

However, not all vampire community members are organized in the same way, as some members also articulate a desire for those pleasures associated with more traditional fan cultures. For example, as argued during chapter 4, Jenny (the previous figurehead of the Vampyre Connexion) reveals how the privileging of subcultural capital over more traditional vampire fan interests does not apply to all members. Jenny notes how she is "more of an old-fashioned vampire fan" and that the community is increasingly moving away from her own cultural interests in the vampire, as interests are transforming from those associated with the traditional literary vampire to those associated with youth and music cultures:

> Jenny: We now have new, younger members and they want different things and we [Jenny and her husband Colin] want it to evolve. That's why we are taking a step back. It has become more gig orientated. That's not why we got it into it. We wanted to visit Strawberry Hill House, the Victorian gothic, masked balls, read Wilkie Collins, because Bram Stoker was that period. People are not as keen on that side any more. (Jenny, Questionnaire)

Jenny's resistance to youth/music inspired activities also has implications on the fourth hierarchy: the hierarchy of leaders. Although Hills notes that this category is particularly problematic, as it suggests a pecking order of leaders among fan groups, this hierarchy is particularly useful in identifying the preferences that are evolving within the community, which appear to be increasingly attached to subcultural involvement. For over ten years, married couple Colin (also known as the Vampyre Master) and Jenny have been responsible for running the Vampyre Connexion. They are two extremely well-established figureheads within the vampire community and their relationship with MorbidFrog (social secretary) is extremely close, as they increasingly share responsibility between the roles (as well as the other people on the committee). More recently, a change in leadership at the Vampyre Connexion has occurred, with Colin and Jenny stepping down from their positions and moving to Wales, allowing younger members to organize the community so that it may evolve.

Although the leadership of the Vampyre Connexion has been left open, indirectly, MorbidFrog has continued to organize and publicize events, write for the fanzine *Dark Nights*, and send out all online information, such as the reminders for monthly meetings. Therefore, although she does not explicitly fit the role of leader, she is the online (and to an extent offline) face of the Vampyre Connexion. Therefore, the hierarchy of what MacDonald refers to as leadership (but in this case might be more appropriately termed *organizer*) contributes once again to MorbidFrog's celebrification. The changeover in organization continues to reveal how members of the vampire community are increasingly favoring dress and subcultural activities in place of the more traditional fan pursuits, and those members who are more interested in intellectual or literary fan pursuits are quite literally taking their interests elsewhere.

CLIQUES, FRAGMENTS, AND EXISTING ON THE OUTSIDE

As the transferal of organizational duties at the Vampyre Connexion illustrates, the vampire community is not necessarily as neatly organized around this model of subcultural celebrity as it first appears. As members have different interests, and while most members gravitate around taking part in an identity subculture (and a celebrity), not all members center around this principle. As MacDonald's final hierarchy of venue will demonstrate, there are further examples of fragmentation occurring within the community. It is this hierarchy that both consolidates MorbidFrog's privileged position within the community and indeed reveals her celebrification, but it also reveals the tensions and cliques of the wider community and how this model may be problematized.

According to MacDonald (1998), the hierarchy of venue describes the powerful role a fan possesses when she hosts events in her home or organizes conventions. MacDonald notes that this can also extend to venues online, for example, if a fan has ownership of e-mail lists, or creates web pages. When applying this principle to MorbidFrog, it is immediately evident that it is in this position that she is most effective, and it is through her collective social networking site venues that she experiences the most disproportionate, non-reciprocal position within the community, leading to her celebrification.

MorbidFrog has constructed a recognizable virtual image of herself via various online codes. First, her unusual name, MorbidFrog, which relates to her love of both the macabre and frogs and (as she notes) is also a light-hearted reference to her French nationality, is highly identifiable and is used repeatedly in all e-mail and web addresses. Similarly, the image of a frog as her cursor (on her MySpace profile) and the employment of a custom-made black, red, and gray color-schemed background on both MySpace and LiveJournal together forge a kind of MorbidFrog brand identity. Similarly, her tagline on Facebook and MySpace, "Everyday is Halloween," is also her signature on the Vampyre Connexion Yahoo e-mail group, which reads as if it were a commercial e-mail signature: "Everyday is Halloween, To know everything I get up to visit http://morbidfrog.livejournal.com."

MorbidFrog is also responsible for distributing an extremely high volume of information to the vampire community, which has resulted in her prestigious position within the subculture. Each month she creates a three-page Vampyre Connexion events spreadsheet, which is both printed and hosted on her website. She also sends out weekly e-mails to the Vampyre Connexion Yahoo group, updating members with up-to-the-minute information on events, cheap tickets, and various reminders for vampire meetups. Similarly, she posts events on her Facebook page, her MySpace bulletin board, and entries on the Friends page of LiveJournal in the hope to capture all members of the community, regardless of their network. In turn, this has led to her well-known status among the community, as the vast majority of members either know her personally or have received information from her.

In fact, her own comments regarding her highly recognizable online username, MorbidFrog, suggest that this has become something of a professional stage name. During interviews, she discussed an encounter with the mass-mediated celebrity Eileen Daly, who played the lead female in the vampire film *Razor Blade Smile*. MorbidFrog noted that due to her own increased exposure as a result of her online activities, there was a mutual acceptance and acknowledgement of their different types of fame, revealing an interesting example of broad and narrow casting celebrities. MorbidFrog notes how she was surprised and pleased when the actress discovered that she was indeed *the* MorbidFrog.

> MorbidFrog: I love it when people come up to me and say, "Are you MorbidFrog?" A few weeks ago I went to Salvation Books' launch party and I met Eileen Daly, the actress from *Razor Blade Smile*. I've known Eileen for years as she goes to the same club as me, but she always knew me as Cecile, and then she said "Oh, *you* are actually MorbidFrog." I got all excited. (Individual Interview 3)

MorbidFrog frequently uses LiveJournal to document her offline activities. Her journal catalogs her participation in the London goth and vampire scene; entries include her experiences at alternative bring-and-buy sales, various graveyard walks, clubbing at numerous locations, and her travels further afield to various alternative festivals in Germany, Austria, and Venice. The amount of comments and interest that MorbidFrog's online postings receive also reflect not only her position but the recognition of her status by the rest of the community and the amount of people who attend her online venues.

For instance, while conducting group and individual interviews, numerous respondents referred directly to MorbidFrog and intimated a reliance on her information postings about events and more generally on the blogs and journal entries that she writes. For example, Ruth explained that the only reason that she signed up to LiveJournal was so that she could read and contribute to other people's pages: "I have a LiveJournal account purely so I can comment on other people's . . . If MorbidFrog writes something she has been doing then I will comment, if they are feeling down then I will say I'm thinking of you" (Group Interview 2). Similarly, MorbidFrog describes one incident that demonstrates the extent to which other community members rely on her information and read her journal, as they may quite literally lurk on her LiveJournal page:

> MorbidFrog: I have a strange readership. I always get people that I don't know coming up to me. Like last week I was at a gig and this girl said to me, "Hi, I am your online stalker. I'm not on LiveJournal, but I always read you to see what's going on." (Individual Interview 3)

As is evident from the previous statement from her "online stalker," MorbidFrog's online popularity may be consolidated by her offline status, but it is her use of online venue that has actually extended her disproportionate reach among the community. Other members of the alternative community that MorbidFrog has not met in face-to-face environments actually recognize her from her online profile. Therefore, MorbidFrog's subcultural celebrity status may be closely mapped to her offline social position, but it is her use of social networks that have made her so widely recognizable.

In contrast, despite social networking sites' potential to contribute to the mediation of subcultural celebrities, some of the tools and media that are increasingly being used by the more high-profile members of the community have been rejected by other members on the grounds that they foster cliques and friendship hierarchies. At this point it is important to point out that these comments have not been directed at MorbidFrog, as, on the contrary, all of the comments that have been made throughout this research concerning MorbidFrog have been extremely positive (validating her respected position in the community). Instead, negative comments have been more generally directed at users of the social networking site LiveJournal, revealing that social networking venues may be integral to the mediation of subcultural celebrity but are also purposefully rejected by some members of the community. Several members of the community have expressed negative views about LiveJournal, suggesting that it is particularly cliquey and can be rather isolating for those who do not use the site and thus produces a "cyberer than thou" effect. Much like the phrase "gother than thou," which derives from a satirical view of extreme goth lifestyle and the maintenance of subcultural standards and ethics, some vampire community members have expressed their frustration with LiveJournal users, describing them as a mini-community and an impenetrable clique.

This sense of fragmentation and consequent isolation is not surprising due to the very nature of social media. Although members of the vampire community have discussed instances where they have met new friends online, the main purpose of social networking sites is to allow users to take existing relationships from face-to-face settings and move them onto the Internet. Hodkinson's early discussion of social media site Netgoth also reveals what he terms as a subsubculture online (2002: 191), demonstrating this fragmentation occurs within wider subcultural communities. Not only is there a sense of community online, but there also seem to be subgroups operating within the wider subcultural structure. As Hodkinson notes, with many more members of the subculture recently migrating online, the sense of exclusivity has decreased, but as the debate around LiveJournal reveals, this has not entirely dissolved. Therefore, by their very nature, social networks can foster cliques and friendship hierarchies within the community. This is exacerbated by the fact that people are using a combination of different technologies, including Facebook, LiveJournal, and MySpace. This sense of fragmentation was highlighted throughout various interviews and group interviews, as Rebecca articulates:

Rebecca: There is definitely a fragmentation within the community, and it's still very cliquey. There is a group online that's very obvious; they will friend you, but you will never really be part of the group. (Group Interview 2)

Anna: I have looked at LiveJournal, but I really, really don't want to get involved in that. MorbidFrog writes on it every day, and that's great if you go out all the time, and her accounts are really good fun to read. But you read other people and you think, why would you bother? They are boring. There is also a question of privacy. I have heard all sorts of massive rows going on LiveJournal. People defriending each other and having rows online. These are people that see each other every few weeks!

Matilda: Isn't it sad to do that kind of stuff in the abstract. (Group Interview 2)

As well as cultivating feelings of cliques and hierarchies within the subculture, the recent change in how people use the Internet, termed the egocentric shift, also has implications for members who are not deeply immersed in the community's activities on a daily basis. As the following example reveals, this shift can result in their further isolation and even detachment from the grouping. A London Vampyre Group committee member posted a message on the vampire e-mail group VEIN (Vampire Exchange Information Network), requesting the community's feedback over their decision to close the e-group. This immediately sparked a series of responses from the community, with many people suggesting that VEIN had served its purpose, and that social networking sites were actually more successful in maintaining the community. VEIN was consequently closed in 2008.

Writing as the moderator for this egroup, I will remind everyone that we considered the future of the VEIN egroup some months ago and I stated that I had come to the conclusion that the days of this circle as a networking group were numbered, as the number of posts had dwindled and all that the group was being used for was as a noticeboard for information that was appearing elsewhere anyway. . . . We had a good run with this one and some good laughs, discussions and arguments, but it's now time to call it a day and I am closing posting rights for everyone. (LVMG17 e-mail, 2007)

However, this shift does have implications for those members who may not use online social networks or perhaps exist on the outskirts of the community, as they experience an increased sense of separation from the subcultural community. The following response from a vampire community and VEIN member exemplifies this sense of isolation, revealing that the net does not seem to be cast that wide, and these online venues that are championed by some may also be the source of isolation for others:

> I have to admit to not attending any specific vampyre group for about three years now. Yet still follow VEIN on the off chance of making any of the more general events that are advertised. If VEIN is going to close then can someone point me to the alternative/individual sites that are more commonly used now? (Anon, female, e-mail, 2007)

Therefore, a focus on more egocentric social networks may have led to the increased participation for some members of the community and also paved the way for subcultural celebrities to emerge. Other members (i.e., those who do not have a high level of interaction online or do not participate offline) may find themselves a little lost in cyberspace.

This sense of community fragmentation also continues in face-to-face contexts, as the type of events and venues that vampire community members attend may also be deemed exclusive by some members of the community, especially considering that many of these events are planned online (i.e., on LiveJournal). As the contrasting experiences outlined below suggest, the attendance of smaller, more select groupings or cliques held at private venues can both reinforce one's position in the subculture—and hence contribute to the privileged position of members, such as MorbidFrog—and also reveal that such activities may not extend to the experiences of all members of the group.

> MorbidFrog: I have never had so many truly good friends. I don't see them just at community events, I see them outside of that. We go to each other's houses for dinner; we go to exhibitions; it's such a genuine scene. . . . I remember a few years ago when I had to move house. I just put a post on LiveJournal saying I am moving on Sunday morning if anyone can help me. On Sunday morning, ten people were outside my door! (Individual Interview 3)

> Beth: They send out messages about where they are going to meet up . . . most people have got theirs on private or "friends only" on LiveJournal. . . . I have made acquaintances online, but I find socializing extremely difficult and I wouldn't say that anyone's on a friend level, because they all get invited to each other's houses and no one has ever invited me, so I would say I have made acquaintances as opposed to friends. (Individual Interview 4)

MorbidFrog is articulating how online and offline venues have contributed to her extremely positive experiences within the community. The smaller, everyday lifestyle events that she discusses suggest that she has an extremely deep immersion in the subculture, and such daily participation provides a sense of belonging to a group of real friends. In contrast, Beth articulates quite a different experience of the subculture, as she suggests that the more intimate events quite often do not extend to her, describing people that she has met as acquaintances as opposed to friends, and revealing once again that the vampire community is not a unified community.[4]

Therefore, through the hierarchies of knowledge, access, fandom level, leaders, and venue, this case study has revealed how in some rare cases, through the daily description of their ordinary practices, vampire community members may experience heightened levels of intimacy and a disproportionate relationship in the community that can lead to their celebrification. It has been argued that the positioning of high-profile members has become more transparent through the egocentric shift and the increased emphasis on user participation on social media sites. It has also been suggested that new media technologies—specifically, sites such as Facebook, LiveJournal, and MySpace—are increasingly changing the media landscape, forcing researchers to questions the rigid definitions of celebrity in order to find a new direction (Hills 2006). However, such online social media have also played a crucial role in identifying the fragmentation within the community, revealing discrepancies in member's experiences, suggesting that not all members are organized neatly around such concepts of celebrity. So while there may be emergent subcultural celebrities around whom community members can exist, this model does not necessarily extend to all.

Moreover, the discussion so far has focused on the five key hierarchies that can be useful in explaining the emergence of subcultural celebrities. However, MacDonald's model does not place enough emphasis on individuals' creativity, or on what Hills terms subcultural/niche mediation. As the following section will demonstrate, dress and the fashioning of subcultural style plays an absolutely crucial role in determining status and position within the community.

THE HIERARCHY OF PERFORMANCE

MorbidFrog engages daily in a fully elaborated sartorial vampire identity, dressing in outfits that vary from Victoriana mourning costume to steampunk and ethereal poses. She engages in a subcultural style of dress at home, work, and social events, in and outside of the subculture. She may have to curtail her outfits for practicalities, such as cycling to work, but continues to engage her vampire identity every day. Her image is predominately associated with the historical gothic and morbid beauty aesthetic, with hints of burlesque glamour. She has long black hair, cut into vintage, retro style Bettie Page bangs. Her makeup produces a gothic combination of ivory skin and dark black eyeliner, accentuating the eyes, often with black swirls stenciled around her long, thick eyelash extensions and ivory-powdered cheekbones. Her voluptuous figure is usually corseted, accentuating her waist, and she wears long, usually black skirts (with or without bustle). The overall look is usually black (with hints of gothic plum or green) set off with a combination of silver and black jewelry, lace gloves, Edwardian-inspired fans, parasols, Victorian cocktail hats, and, in most instances, fangs.

MorbidFrog also has three vampire-related tattoos, including a frog with fangs, a vampire bat and coffin, and an angel of death, complete with black cloak and scythe, which was inspired by an image from *Buffy the Vampire Slayer Magazine*. She is now intending to cover her entire body with tattooed ivy, as she loves the aesthetic of ivy creeping and climbing over gravestones in cemeteries. She notes, "It's beautiful when you see a gravestone covered in ivy. So now I am covering myself in just that!" (MorbidFrog, Individual Interview 3). MorbidFrog's performative identity also extends to the decoration of her Camden-based home. For example, her living room includes a gothic art exhibition poster; an assortment of crosses, including an intricately designed handmade crucifix made by her own hand; Halloween pumpkins; a bookcase filled with dusty books; deep red roses; candles; a taxidermy owl and squirrel; and a stone gargoyle. Her bedroom is black, with black bed sheets, and the ceiling is entwined with a forest of flower chains that fill the entire area above her bed. The kitchen contains black, gothic-inspired dinner plates, skeleton mugs, and historical wine chalices.

The fashioning of MorbidFrog's subcultural style is also continued online. For instance, MorbidFrog's MySpace profile page layout is designed with a gothic black-and-red color scheme; she has also used customized gothic graphics and selected a pagan contact table. The images on her Facebook profile reveal a range of vampire-related aesthetics, such as images of her posing at various gravestones, both alone and with friends. She is clad in gothic apparel and appears to be presenting historical gothic images from romance/seduction, gothic elegance, horror, ethereal poses, and, more recently, steampunk. The photographs reveal her extremely varied sense of style (but constrained within the limits of the subculture), including antique Victorian clothing, more cyber influenced PVC outfits, and sartorial tributes

Figures 21–22 Danse Macabre: The Noble Blood Vampire Ball, Belgium, 2011. Photographs: Soulstealer Photography (SoulStealer.co.uk)

Figure 23 White Mischief Halloween Ball: Ghost in the Machine, London, 2011. Photograph: Soulstealer Photography (SoulStealer.co.uk)

to the steampunk movement as well as specific outfits that represent vampire iconography. In one photograph, which was taken for the Vampyre Connexion's Halloween party, she presents herself as an actual vampire or horror icon. Her eyes have been blacked out; her mouth is open as if she was howling, and blood drips down from her fangs.

> MorbidFrog: I look at a lot of historical books of costume, antiques fairs. I have made my own wings out of tights and a coat hanger. It's such an eclectic taste; I don't like wearing the same thing twice. I like adding flowers to my hair, or spiders to my hat. Everything around you can be used in your outfit. (Individual Interview 3)

Figures 24–25 Thé Asylum, Lincoln, 2011. Photographs: Soulstealer Photography (SoulStealer.co.uk)

Through consideration of the hierarchy of performance in both online and face-to-face contexts, it is evident that MorbidFrog is consistently elaborate in her performance and holds a position at the top of this hierarchy. Social networking sites allow her to fashion an extremely elaborate identity online, which reflects her offline life, allowing her to show off her gothic vampire creativity. Her performative identity has led to her widespread recognition, and her diverse online readership has given her an increased sense of intimacy, as people who have never even met her desire to read her journal entries and view her photography. As the following statement by a fellow vampire community member illustrates, MorbidFrog's fashioning of a subcultural style has played an integral part in her celebrification. She is a style leader who is known disproportionately by members of the community, and typical of celebrity culture, others desire to replicate aspects of her style and seek inspiration in her performance:

> Ronita: In the community you have people like MorbidFrog, who look ridiculously amazing all the time, and when I see her and how fabulous she looks, I am tempted to dress up more. I might get more into it and become a lot darker. When you see MorbidFrog, she never looks the same twice; she always does such creative things with her clothes and makeup. (Individual Interview 1)

Although, as Ronita points out, many members of the community are organized around subcultural celebrity, the performative pleasures that have been integral to MorbidFrog's celebrification are not shared by all members of the group. As the following discussion between members of the London Vampyre Group reveals, the vampire community might offer pleasures in standing out from the mainstream, but some members feel compelled to adhere to the vampire front. Therefore, in some rare cases, members may actually prefer to dress in a less alternative fashion but fear the consequences of not appropriating the desired gothic aesthetic. This indicates that there are varying levels of participation occurring within the community because not all members are gravitating around performance and presenting cult objects to the same degree, as some members of the community (albeit a small proportion) do not necessarily equate their vampire interests with dress.

> Lou: I would wear baggy, skatery-type stuff to LVG events sometimes, but I feel a bit self-conscious wearing that to the LVG meeting in case people are thinking, "Who's that in the denim?"
>
> Lyla: The LVG are not quite as bad as Vampyre Connexions. I have gone into the Connexions and not had time to change into my alternate clothes, and people have not actually spoken to me as much as they usually do.

Rebecca: I have seen that with our own people at the LVG in the past, where we have had somebody come to an event dressed very smartly, or in clothes that are not alternative at all, and they have been pushed away and told that they shouldn't be here. I find that strange because we say that we accept anybody . . . but what is also strange is if you look at LiveJournal, the amount of grief some people give to those who aren't alternative who want to come to events. They are really saying that we don't want that type of person to come along. Well, why not? (Group Interview 1)

Therefore, going back to the research questions posed at the end of chapter 3, this chapter has found that processes of celebrification are occurring within the vampire community. In rare instances, members who engage daily in highly elaborated vampire masquerade, both online and offline, can become subcultural celebrities. MorbidFrog's celebrification is due to her highly elaborate vampire performance and online/offline immersion in subcultural lifestyle. MorbidFrog has procured knowledge of the subculture and demonstrated an extremely high level of subcultural participation at both larger scale community events and smaller, more exclusive groupings. She fulfills roles such as information provider and membership representative, providing access to the new and lesser known members of the community. Her online social networking sites, such as LiveJournal, Facebook, and MySpace, and her events list are frequently visited venues, which reveal her diverse readership and prestigious position. Her extremely identifiable style, both online (through displaying photography) and offline (through sartorial engagement) has culminated in the emergence of a highly recognizable MorbidFrog brand identity.

This chapter has also found that while the hierarchies of knowledge, fandom level, access, leadership, venue, and performance might be useful in identifying the process of vampire celebrification, use of this model in isolation would be problematic, as this would preclude wider understandings of the organization of the community that includes cliques and members who may not gravitate around subcultural celebrity. For the majority of the vampire community, the pleasures of belonging to a group of likeminded others is key; however, some members struggle to fit into the vampire front, whether feeling pressures to adopt certain styles of dress or, as Beth articulates, not fitting into exclusive cliques in online and face-to-face venues.

−7−

Conclusions

Over the course of this book, my aims were to establish how members of the vampire community draw on and commodify the legend of the vampire in their everyday life, and to unearth the more complex driving forces and motivating factors behind vampire community membership. Along the way, I have met many fascinating people, whose insights have been invaluable. However, I have also had to dispel many myths regarding vampire culture, which ranged from my own initial misinterpretations of the community (documented in chapter 2) to wider misconceptions regarding the true nature of the vampire community and the types of people that enlist.

In fact, during this research I have occasionally come up against ill-informed opinions that deem the vampire community to be, at best, a kind of sensationalist freak show and at worst, a dangerous cult (I have detailed the hurtful remarks and ill treatment of community members at various points throughout this book). For instance, during one of the early London Vampyre Group meetings at the Intrepid Fox, I was approached by a man called Wolfbane, who struck up a conversation with me on the premise that he was a long-standing member of the group. At this initial stage in my research I was rather unfamiliar with group members and therefore assumed that he was genuine, but as the conversation progressed, I began to realize he was not a member of the community at all. Rather, upon seeing the vampire community meeting poster, he had wandered into the upstairs bar hoping to witness some sanguinarian activity. Having bought himself a drink and taken a few moments to soak up the scene (which included people standing around the bar in their finest vampire outfits, drinking, chatting, listening to music, and catching up with old friends), he was clearly underwhelmed by the ordinariness of the community meeting and exclaimed with disappointment, "I thought you lot would be slitting yourselves and drinking blood by now. I think blood is fantastic in sex." He then promptly exited the venue, noticeably dissatisfied that he had not been privy to any acts of blood drinking.

Similarly, after completing this research, a sprinkling of documentary film-makers showed an interest in translating the subject matter into film and television formats (the completion of my research coincided with the recent hype and commercial success of vampires in mainstream media, which made this study a particularly attractive project at the time). However, despite some genuine interest in the subcultural element of the community from one independent television company, the majority of media interest was far more sensationalistic in its approach. Therefore, after endless debates with producers about blood drinking, and infuriating statements—such as "But there must be those who drink blood; how do we gain access to them?", "What about devil worship, then? Could we get some shots of them chanting, perhaps even doing some kind of sacrifice?", and "Do they have vampire weddings, where they drink blood from chalices?"—I decided to write this book.

Needless to say, such misconceptions about the vampire community have attached rather distasteful connotations to the subculture, and as one member summarizes, this has made the community rather difficult to maintain (Demondaz, Group Interview 6). Even members of neighboring subcultures, such as the goth scene, occasionally feel the need to completely disassociate themselves from the vampire community for fear of being tarred with the same, unsavory brush. For instance, during this research, vampire community members explained how some of their goth friends purposely distance themselves from vampire affiliation for a number of reasons, ranging from viewing vampires as something of a gothic cliché to their desire to avoid the negative associations of blood cultism. Jillian Venters, author of *Gothic Charm School* (2009), picks up on this tension during the first episode of her book's video edition.[1] During the video, The Lady of the Manners explains the origins of the goth subculture and states that there is often a tendency for goths to avoid associations with vampires. She states, "Goth is also an aesthetic that mixes funereal elegance with black humor, B-movie kitsch, and a healthy dose of vampires. I know, I know, we all want to avoid that cliché, but admit it, you have vampire books on your bookshelf, too" (Episode 1). Similarly, in 2008 the desire to loosen links between goth and vampire communities was also satirized in the adult animation television show *South Park.* During the episode "Ungroundable" (12:14), the goth kids of South Park Elementary become increasingly frustrated at being continually mistaken for vampire kids. The goth kids describe the school's brand new subculture as "Justin (Timberlake) and Britney (Spears) wannabes," who since the release of the *Twilight* movies suddenly "think it's cool to dress like us."[2]

While a desire for separation and even segregation between subcultural groupings certainly does not extend to all members of the goth community, and many vampire members are indeed self-proclaimed goths, this friction does reveal the complex predicament that vampire community members find themselves in, which may even threaten the future of the group. During interviews, one member of the vampire community explained how he found himself turning to wider subcultural groupings, namely steampunk, because the connotations were simply not as damaging:

> Demondaz: I think the steampunk scene will actually be bigger than the vampire scene. Although vampire lifestylers have been around for twenty years or so, it's actually quite a hard scene to maintain interest in. It's an uphill battle, as some people like to read unsavory aspects into the vampire scene, but I don't think they can read unsavory aspects into steampunk enthusiast groups. Take my own mother, for example, when I show her vampire photo shoots she says, "Oh, I don't like that, you're all covered in blood." But when I show her steampunk shoots, where I am dressed as well-to-do gentleman, well, she likes that! My money would be on steampunk blowing the vampire scene out of the water. (Individual Interview 6)

Therefore, although I do not want to end this book on a negative note and certainly do not want to position the vampire community as a powerless, victimized group (on the contrary, as discussed elsewhere, the vampire community is a space to express strong feminine ideas and to fashion a distinctive individual style that reflects women's choice and self-confidence), it is important to point out the complexities and difficulties that community members face.

These damaging myths not only have implications on the future of the subculture but are also integral to my own motivations for wanting to write this book. Although I am not claiming to have discovered all there is to know about vampire culture, and as with any empirical audience study, research of this kind is difficult and can often raise as many questions as it answers, I hope that at the very least this book might assist outsiders in understanding the real nature of a subculture that is largely unknown to most people. Conducting research into the vampire community is important, as essentially it is precisely the intricate workings of the community, from group hierarchies to identity politics, as opposed to shocking accounts of blood drinking and biting that are the truly fascinating topics here. Therefore, what I have attempted to do throughout this book is to present the vampire community as I have found them since 2007, focusing on the day-to-day running of the community and the aspects of lifestyle that are so often neglected in wider accounts of vampire communities in favor of shock tactics and more sensationalist pre-occupations. The discussion will now briefly reframe the material discussed in previous chapters and highlight the significance of this book.

THE COMMODIFICATION OF VAMPIRE CULTURE

Returning to the research questions that underpin this research, chapter 4 has revealed that the community's relationship with the vampire is maintained through commodity purchase. Members can purchase a number of commodities, including custom-made fangs that are fitted to the teeth, custom-made corsetry, Victorian/Edwardian clothing, jewelry, gothic bed sheets, dinner plates, ornamental crosses, taxidermy ornaments, gothic art, decorative gargoyles, gothic/vampire/fairy dolls, and more. Vampire community members can also commodify their own arts and crafts, including steampunk, neo-Victorian, and elegant gothic Lolita jewelry and accessories and use this productivity to generate income for their own small businesses.

Chapter 5 then identified the predominant underlying gendered discourses that operate within the vampire community. The discussion drew upon the work of Joanne Hollows (2003), in the "Masculinity of Cult," which examined the use of the "sleazo movie theatre" in the emergence of Midnight Movie and the gendering of traditional, pre-Internet and DVD cult consumption as masculine. This chapter argued that because Hollows's work is framed historically, there is a need to update research in this area of female cult fans and their position within fan culture, as significant developments have taken place since women adopted the position of being "culturally one of the boys" (Thornton 1995, in Hollows 2003).

This research has developed this debate and has explored how the women of the vampire community have continued to draw on gothic/ vampire media in the twenty-first century, so that they may also position themselves outside of feminized mass culture. However, rather paradoxically, women are not positioning themselves as one of the boys but draw on particularly feminine patterns of production, such as those associated with dress, makeup, hairstyling, accessorizing, and even decorating their homes. By reimagining historical identities that celebrate feminine curves and the hourglass figure with a more diaphanous complexion, women separate themselves from more modern mainstream constructs of femininity. I argued that for some women, dressing differently reveals feelings of *outsiderdom* and not fitting in to more mainstream aspects of society. For others, it is an aesthetic decision, as fashioning neo-Victorian styles of dress is associated with a love for the historical. Such dress practices are also tied to size and *shapism* issues, as corsets and bustled skirts flatter the fuller, voluptuous figure. For others, alternative dress may reveal more direct ideologies of power and of women's attitudes toward modern beauty ideals and social norms.

Chapter 5 also demonstrated that while women were generally presenting vampire identities in line with Dunja Brill's (2008) cult of femininity, conflicting experiences do exist, as women use steampunk to fashion more androgynous styles that allow them a level of freedom from the hyperfeminine, morbid beauty aesthetic. Chapter 6 then developed these inconsistencies and revealed that the community does not exist as a cohesive place. Through case study analysis of style leader MorbidFrog, the discussion explained that the community is both a collective community with a shared group identity and a place for fragmentation. The varying technologies selected by members (Facebook, MySpace, LiveJournal), the cliques formed on each of the subsequent sites, and the "cyberer than thou" complex, all work to demonstrate that the community is as fragmented online as it is offline (exemplified by the fragmented groupings of the London Vampyre Group, Vampyre Connexion, and the London Vampire Meetup Group). Therefore, although the commodification of the vampire is central to members' experiences, this commodification can also be rather alienating. Women who are rich in subcultural capital, who are quite often younger, time-rich members that have the freedom to indulge in lifestyle activities on a perpetual basis, may have a rather different experience of the community to those who can only dress up for some events. Subsequently, members that cannot make their own clothes and cannot afford or simply refuse to purchase such commodities can feel disenfranchised.

Therefore, in bringing this book to a close, having summarized the major findings of this research, it is now important to consider the significance of this study and any new research avenues that have arisen as a result of its completion. First, after spending considerable time immersed in vampire culture, I can only conclude that further research into how wider communities use dress and commodities to perform identity is crucial. The timely emergence of the steampunk subculture that coincided with my research of the vampire community has already allowed me to gain some insights into steampunk, and how issues of class and British national identity are important factors in identity construction. Further questions must now be raised in order to expand upon these issues. For instance, how might online media facilitate the diffusion of style across steampunks? Are these communities organized around high-profile style leaders? How are clothes linked to Britishness and ideas of class elevation? Similarly, how do other emerging fan communities, such as cosplayers,[3] use dress to express their love for their fan object?

Second, this study opens up wider lines of inquiry into the relationship between fan cultures and subcultures, and how they are changing in entity, as the vampire community reveals a convergence of the two. For many, fandom is not what it used to be. As the vampire community demonstrates, not all fan communities need to share a simplistic love for a text, as the media function as a starting point for playing with one's identity. In a wider sense, fandom is increasingly aligned with lifestyle choices, and media texts can now be seen as a jumping off point, as these are not just fan performances but provide a springboard for insights into the self. In fact, the term *fan* is quite problematic when used in relation to such hybrid communities (such as the vampires, steampunks, and cosplayers), as the increasing focus on lifestyle activities and dress has created a distance from the original text (i.e., vampire fiction), which makes the term seem rather imposed. That is not to suggest that the vampire community does not include fans and aficionados of the vampire, but for many, their interest in the gothic and historical vampire are, in effect, lived out. These interests in the vampire are not lived out in the sense that members are engaging in any real-life vampire fantasies or bloodletting activities but in the sense that they are revealing their interests through vampire styling on the body, online, and in their homes.

However, it is important to keep in mind that although for many the relationship with the text is becoming increasingly ingrained in lifestyle activities, fan performance is not a new phenomenon. For example, in the 1970s, fans of the *Rocky Horror Picture Show* generated this performative nature, as the text was transformed into a participatory cult event and fans played an active role in the cinema. Bruce Austin (2008) outlines the types of participation that fans of Rocky Horror engage in, from audience members shouting questions out to the characters, adding lines of dialogue, using props such as flashlights and water pistols, to "more extreme forms of participation," which include the "public commitment" of costuming themselves like characters from the narrative (2008: 400). It is also important to note that this study is not suggesting that recent changes in fan communities have transformed all fandoms into performative subcultures; obviously, traditional fan communities still exist. For example, *Dr. Who* has a strong following of female fans who engage closely with the text and do not engage in dress practices to the same degree as we have seen throughout this book.

Nevertheless, this book demonstrates that the nature of fans' engagement with the text is changing, as people are increasingly taking their fandom into different contexts and reimagining the film or television show's diegesis. This reimagining is not limited to dress and lifestyle commodities (as demonstrated by the vampire community) but also extends to the various ways that fans interact with their fandom in everyday life. These include the attendance of horror festivals, such as *Dead by Dawn*, the "squeeing"[4] of fangirls on the Internet, the creation of fan-made films and their exhibition online, and the virtual living room environments created by fans online, so that they can watch programs together and post messages to each other, regardless of geography (Cherry 2009). Therefore the significance of this book far exceeds a monograph of a single community, as this research is not just an investigation into women who like to dress up in a neo-Victorian style of clothing and wear vampire teeth; it is a study of how fan cultures are changing in entity.

As this study has demonstrated, further research into the use of dress and wider commodities within fan and subcultural communities is crucial, as dress can reveal pleasures in standing out from society, dressing differently to the mainstream, and carving out an identity that reveals individuality but also commitment to a group. Clothes can also signal isolation, loneliness, and fragmentation. They can mark out high-profile fans and signal celebrification and identify those with more carnivalesque, part-time pleasures. They can reveal a fascination that goes back to childhood, which has been honed and refined in adulthood. The selection of garments can reveal a rejection of modern beauty standards, be used to demonstrate strong feminist agendas by some, and be denounced by others, and reveal alternative imagined histories.

Notes

CHAPTER 1 TWENTY-FIRST-CENTURY VAMP

1. See Catherine Spooner's discussion of "Undead Fashion: 1990s Style and the Perennial Return to Goth," in *Fashioning Gothic Bodies* (2004).
2. For more details, see The Museum at FIT, *Gothic Dark Glamour*, <www3.fitnyc.edu/museum/gothic/> accessed September 19, 2011.
3. For more details, see *Illamasqua*, <www.illamasqua.com> accessed October 12, 2011.
4. See Henry Jenkins's research on the Matrix and Transmedia Storytelling in *Convergence Culture* (2008).
5. For more details, see *HBO Shop*, <www.store.hbouk.com/?v=hbo-uk_shows_true-blood> accessed September 5, 2011.
6. For more details, see *Etsy,* <www.etsy.com> accessed January 5, 2011.
7. For more details, see *Zazzle,* <www.zazzle.com> accessed January 5, 2011.
8. For more details, see Resistance Gallery, *Fangtasia London: True Blood Vampire Club*, <www.fangtasialondon.blogspot.com> accessed January 5, 2011.

CHAPTER 2 INTERVIEWING VAMPIRES

1. Robbie Drake's company is Blood Red FX. He is a makeup artist and special effects expert.
2. With the possible exception of my sister, who did have an interest in alternative fashion as a teenager; but this was a rather brief period and one that I was too young to observe firsthand.
3. There are obviously wider subcultural communities in London, but these three are of particular interest.
4. An acronym that refers to crossover communities: bondage and discipline, dominance and submission, sadism and masochism.
5. I recruited using online and offline platforms, inserting flyers and questionnaires into the members' copies of the Vampyre Connexion's journal *Dark Nights* and the London Vampyre Group's *Chronicles*. I also attended events, handing out questionnaires to capture people who were not active members but who nevertheless attended events, and I circulated digital questionnaires

online, using my professional account with SurveyMonkey, the online survey website.

6. I distributed fifty-four questionnaires (of which forty-two were fully completed). These questionnaires collected some quantitative data, which was coded and imported into SPSS (Statistical Package for Social Sciences) for analysis. I ensured that I distributed consent forms, which allowed participants to decide how they would like to be referred to during this book (ranging from the option of anonymity to online alias and birth name). The forms also requested that participants disclosed any social networking sites they used, and their profile details. They were specifically asked if I could observe their profile pages and use portions of my findings in my research. This approach was deliberately designed to counteract ethical problems of online research and the issues of obtaining informed consent.

7. For the sake of clarity, and in order to evidence the representative nature of this research, it is useful to outline the vampire community's size. Although there is no way to exhaustively investigate the number of women who have a fascination with vampires that are currently living in London, I can ascertain that there are approximately 100 fully signed-up, active female vampire community members in the capital. According to figures provided by club secretaries, the longest running community, the London Vampyre Group (LVG), has sixty-five active female members, the Vampyre Connexion (VC) has twenty-five active female members, and the London Vampire Meetup Group (LVMG) has twenty active female members, bringing the grand total to 110. Although there are 110 fully signed-up members, there is a substantial amount of crossover between the three London-based vampire organizations, and some members frequent all three groups; therefore, the real number of members is actually closer to 100. Out of the approximately 100 possible candidates, fifty-four respondents returned a completed or partially completed questionnaire. However, only forty-two questionnaires were completed to an acceptable standard (i.e., the majority of questions had been answered). Therefore, the sample achieved can be regarded as particularly representative, as it equates to almost a 50 percent share of the community.

8. The data were then analyzed, aided by NVIVO software package.

9. The meetings were eventually moved from this location due to a number of complaints about staff reception and the unsympathetic nature of the venue.

10. Although I continue to post photographs of myself following mainstream fashion trends, my interest in gothic horror has resulted in the fashioning of various gothic artworks and video clips of my favorite vampire/horror films and television shows.

CHAPTER 3 VAMPIRE FEMININITY AND STATUS

1. Although it is important to note that the community was not always met with animosity and tensions, women often reported positive comments that were made about their outfits from passersby on the street.
2. Although Hollows's work is most useful to draw upon at this point, it is also important to acknowledge that wider scholarly work within subcultures has also readdressed this gender imbalance. Thornton cites the work of Angela McRobbie and Jenny Garber (1977/1997) as particularly important scholars who have both accounted for the position of girls/women within subcultures (Thornton 1997: 6).
3. See *Ax Wound Feminist Horror Zine*, <http://www.axwoundzine.com/> accessed April 19, 2010.
4. See *Pretty Scary*, <http://www.pretty-scary.net> accessed April 19, 2010.
5. Some members of the goth community are also closely affiliated with the fetish industry and BDSM culture; therefore, it is not surprising that sexually ambiguous dress practices may be common for these members of the subculture.

CHAPTER 4 VAMPIRE COMMUNITY PROFILE

1. It is important to point out that not all respondents answered all the questions on each questionnaire. Consequently, the information that is being presented will not always equate to forty-two responses, as in some instances data from participant may be missing.
2. To ensure that this study is representative of the wider experiences of the vampire community, I recruited respondents from diverse age brackets.
3. Wicca is a modern pagan religion, which translates to the word *witch*. An important aspect of Wiccan religion is concerned with balance and with understanding the universe. Practicing magic (or the ancient spelling, *magick*) is central to their spiritual principles.
4. Name changed to provide anonymity.
5. A form of subcultural dress that originated in Japan and is inspired by the visual *kei* music movement. The style fuses aspects of Lolita and Victorian goth. Dresses are often mini- or knee-length, with full frilly skirts and crinolines paired with long socks.
6. This is a popular steampunk characterization, from the comic of the same name.
7. See next section on vampire media for details of new vampire fiction, such as *Twilight* and *True Blood*.
8. Name changed to provide anonymity.
9. Etsy is a site that sells handmade products; see http://www.etsy.com.

10. Although it is worth noting that with the exception of *Being Human*, these fictions already existed in circulation in their literary form (i.e., the *Vampire Diaries Trilogy* was published in 1991, the *Southern Vampire Mysteries* were published from 2001, *Låt den rätte komma* was published in 2004, and *Twilight* was published in 2005).
11. A series of British romance novels.

CHAPTER 5 FEMININE DISCOURSES

1. Frank Langella, "20 Questions Interview," with Marjorie Rosen, *Playboy* (August 1979).
2. It is important to point out that wider discourses have also been identified, such as those relating to attitudes towards race, class, and religion. However, these discourses have produced less conclusive findings, and although they continue to be important, they were less significant to the community at the time of this research. Therefore, although they will be included in the debate, they will be discussed in less detail, as this research will be led by its findings and will refrain from imposing those discourses that the researcher may consider to be important.
3. *Modding* is a term associated with the steampunk movement. For example, case modding involves the act of customizing laptops/computers/iPods with various steampunk-influenced case designs, making the technology appear as though it has been created in the past, intricately crafted with Victorian cogs, wheels, steam pipes, radio valves, and typewriter keys.
4. *Brass Goggles, The Lighter Side of Steampunk,* <http://www.brassgoggles.co.uk> accessed January 10, 2012.
5. *Steamfashion*, <http://www.community.livejournal.com/steamfashion> accessed January 10, 2012.
6. Name changed to provide anonymity.
7. Name changed to provide anonymity.
8. *Tightlacing* is the practice of wearing a corset that has been tightly laced to achieve an extremely cinched waist and a level of body modification.
9. In minute quantities.
10. It is important to point out that tightlacing and the diaphanous complexion were certainly not standard practices for all women during this period. For example, there are many accounts of corsets being used for medical purposes, and tightlacing was simply not practical for many women outside of the upper or leisured classes. However, these ideals were fashioned by members of the vampire community.
11. Anonymity maintained.

NOTES **133**

12. Ronita is using the term *chav* to describe a youth subculture that is usually pitted against goths, vampires, and similar alternative groups. Chav is a derogatory stereotype used mainly in the UK to describe a group of people who dress in sportswear (often heavily branded tracksuit bottoms, hooded tops, and sneakers) and are inspired by American hip-hop culture. The group is usually negatively depicted by the British media as being working-class delinquents who are often associated with trouble making and antisocial behavior.
13. She can only recall one other mixed-race member of the subculture.
14. Anonymity maintained.

CHAPTER 6 ALTERNATIVE CELEBRITY

1. This is not to suggest that tensions and hierarchical positions are not evident among wider subcultures and fan communities, but these issues do appear to be exacerbated by the hybrid nature of the vampire community, which includes high-profile vampire goths as well as people who are predominantly interested in literary vampires.
2. Hills concedes that MacDonald's work does not deal with "real life fandoms," and consequently adopting her method has various problematic concerns. For instance, although MacDonald suggests that "fans may occupy multiple positions simultaneously" (1998: 138), Hills notes that there is a need to account for exactly how these positions may reinforce one another (2006: 105). Heeding Hills's warnings, this discussion takes into account that MorbidFrog holds multiple positions at once (she has a strong position in all five categories) and the interconnected nature of these positions and the consequent effects on other members.
3. However, it should be noted that MorbidFrog also has access to media personalities, such as the mass-mediated celebrity Eileen Daly, from the vampire film *Razor Blade Smile*, as will be discussed in due course.
4. It must also be noted that, due to her neurological condition, Beth discussed how she finds all social situations rather difficult and therefore may feel more intense feelings of isolation when compared to other members. Nevertheless, feelings of fragmentation and isolation are characteristic of some members of the group.

CHAPTER 7 CONCLUSIONS

1. See Jillian Venters, *Gothic Charm School*, May 29, 2009, <http://youtube.com> accessed May 12, 2011.

2. The motivation behind the goth kids' desire to segregate the two communities was actually due to their struggle to remain alternative and nonconformist amid the vampire hype (post-*Twilight*) as opposed to being concerned with a desire to separate themselves from vampires due to the darker connotations of the group.

3. *Cosplay* has significant communities in Japan and America (among other places) and is a type of sartorial performance art that involves the act of elaborately dressing as a character from a film, TV series, videogame, or anime. These often extremely intricately designed costumes are then exhibited in various different ways, including posting photographs on an online network joined by other cosplayers and dressing for specific conventions (one of the largest events takes place at Tokyo's Harajuku Bridge).

4. *Squeeing* relates to writing online posts that demonstrate fans' intensity of excitement and delight.

Bibliography

Abercrombie, N. and Longhurst, B. (1998), *Audiences: A Sociological Theory of Performance and Imagination*, London: Sage.

Ang, I. (1985), *Watching Dallas: Soap Opera and the Melodramatic Imagination*, London: Methuen.

Angrosino, M. and Mays de Pérez, K. A. (2003), "Rethinking Observation, from Method to Context," in N. K. Denzin and Y. S. Lincoln (eds), *Collecting and Interpreting Qualitative Materials*, London: Sage, 107–54.

Auerbach, N. (1995), *Our Vampires Ourselves*, Chicago: University of Chicago Press.

Austin, B. A. (2008), "Portrait of a Cult Film Audience," in E. Mathijs and X. Mendik (eds), *The Cult Film Reader*, Berkshire: Open University Press McGraw-Hill, 392–402.

Austin, T. (2002), *Hollywood, Hype and Audiences*, Manchester: Manchester University Press.

Bacon-Smith, C. (1992), *Enterprising Women: Television Fandom and the Creation of Popular Myth*, Philadelphia: University of Pennsylvania Press.

Bacon-Smith, C. (2000), *Science Fiction Culture*, Philadelphia: University of Pennsylvania Press.

Bakhtin, M. (1968), *Rabelais and His World,* Cambridge, MA: MIT Press.

Baudrillard, J. (1994), *Simulacra and Simulation*, trans. S. F. Glaser, Ann Arbor: University of Michigan Press.

Beer, B. and Burrows, R. (2007), "Sociology and, of and in Web 2.0: Some Initial Considerations," *Sociological Research Online*, 12/5, <http://www.socresonline.org.uk/12/5/17.html> accessed November 12, 2007.

Behar, R. (1995), "Introduction: Out of Exile," in R. Behar and D. A. Gordon (eds), *Women Writing Culture*, Berkeley: University of California Press, 1–32.

Berenstein, R. (1996), *Attack of the Leading Ladies: Gender Sexuality, and Spectatorship in Classic Horror Cinema*, New York: Columbia University Press.

Berry, S. (2000), "Be Our Brand: Fashion and Personalisation on the Web," in S. Bruzzi and P. Church Gibson (eds), *Fashion Cultures: Theories, Explorations and Analysis*, London: Routledge, 224–42.

Bettelheim, B. (1978), *The Uses of Enchantment: The Meaning and Importance of Fairy Tales*, London: Penguin.

Bobo, J. (1995), *Black Women as Cultural Readers*, New York: Columbia University Press.

Bourdieu, P. (1984), *Distinction: A Social Critique of the Judgement of Taste*, London: Routledge.

Bourdieu, P. (2001), *Masculine Domination*, Cambridge: Polity.

boyd, d. (2008), "Can Social Network Sites Enable Political Action?," *International Journal of Media and Cultural Politics*, 4/2: 241–4.

boyd, d. m. and Ellison, N. B. (2007), "Social Network Sites: Definition, History, and Scholarship," *Journal of Computer-Mediated Communication*, 13/1, <http://jcmc.indiana.edu/vol13/issue1/boyd.ellison.html> accessed November 2, 2007.

Brill, D. (2008), *Goth Culture: Gender, Sexuality and Style*, Oxford: Berg.

Brooker, W. (1998), "Internet Fandom and Continuing Narratives of Star Wars, Blade Runner and Alien," in A. Kuhn (ed.), *Alien Zone II*, London: Verso.

Brooker, W. (2002), *Using the Force: Creativity, Community and Star Wars Fans*, London: Continuum.

Brown, M. E. (1990), *Television and Women's Culture*, London: Routledge.

Buckingham, D. (2008), "Introducing Identity," in D. Buckingham (ed.), *Youth, Identity and Digital Media*, Cambridge, MA: MIT Press, 1–24.

Butler, J. (1990), *Gender Trouble: Feminism and the Subversion of Identity*, London: Routledge.

Butler, J. (1993), *Bodies That Matter: On the Discursive Limits of "Sex,"* New York: Routledge.

Butler, J. (1999), *Gender Trouble: Feminism and the Subversion of Identity*, 2nd ed., New York: Routledge.

Butler, J. (2002), "The Queen of Queer," in R. Alsop, A. Fitzsimons, and K. Lennon (eds), *Theorizing Gender*, Cambridge: Polity.

Butler, R. (2001), "The Moral and Medical Regulation of Sex, Sexualities and Gender," in K. Backett-Milburn and L. McKie (eds), *Constructing Bodies*, London: Palgrave Macmillan.

Byars, J. (1991), *All that Hollywood Allows: Re-Reading Gender in 1950s Melodrama*, London: Routledge.

Cahill, S. and Riley, S. (2001), "Resistances and Reconciliations: Women and Body Art," in A. Guy, E. Green, and M. Banim (eds), *Through the Wardrobe: Women's Relationship with Clothes*, Oxford: Berg.

Campbell, J. and Harbord, J. (1999), "Playing It Again: Citation, Reiteration or Circularity?," *Theory, Culture and Society*, 16/2: 229–41.

Carter, D. (2005), "Living in Virtual Communities: An Ethnography of Human Relationships in Cyberspace," *Information, Communication & Society*, 8/2: 148–67.

Certeau, M. de (1984), *The Practices of Everyday Life*, Berkeley: University of California Press.

Cherry, B. (2001), "Screaming for Release: The Interpretative Activities of Female Horror Film Fans," in J. Petley and S. Chibnall (eds), *British Horror Cinema*, London: Routledge, 42–57.

Cherry, B. (2002), "Refusing to Refuse to Look: Female Viewers of the Horror Film," in M. Jancovich (ed.), *Horror: The Film Reader*, London: Routledge, 169–78.

Cherry, B. (2009), "Viewing Online: The Doctor Who Revival and Fan Audiences," Proceedings for the Transforming Audiences Conference, September 6, 2007, University of Westminster, London.

Cherry, B. and Mellins, M. (2012), "Negotiating the Punk in Steampunk: Subculture, Fashion and Performative Identity," *Punk & Post-Punk*, 1/1: 5–25.

Cicioni, M. (1998), "Male Pair-Bonds and Female Desire in Fan Slash Writing," in C. Harris and A. Alexander (eds), *Theorizing Fandom: Fans, Subculture and Identity*, Hampton: Cresskill, 153–77.

Clover, C. (1992), *Men, Women and Chainsaws: Gender in the Modern Horror Film*, Princeton, NJ: Princeton University Press.

Cohen, A. K. (1955/1997), "A General Theory of Subcultures," in K. Gelder and S. Thornton (eds), *The Subcultures Reader*, 2nd ed., Oxon: Routledge, 50–9.

Cohen, S. (1972), *Folk Devils and Moral Panics,* London: MacGibbon and Kee.

Cohen, S. (1987/1997), "Symbols of Trouble," in K. Gelder and S. Thornton (eds), *The Subcultures Reader,* Oxon: Routledge.

Cohen, S. (2002), *Folk Devils and Moral Panics*, Third Edition, Oxon: Routledge.

Creed, B. (2003), *The Monstrous Feminine: Film, Feminism, Psychoanalysis*, London: Routledge.

Cressey, P. G. (1932), *The Taxi-Dance Hall: A Sociological Study in Commercialised Recreation and City Life*, Chicago: University of Chicago Press.

De Vaus, D. (2002), *Surveys in Social Research*, 5th ed., London: Routledge.

Delis Hill, D. (2004), *As Seen in Vogue*, Lubbock: Texas Tech University Press.

Deuze, M. (2004), "Mark Deuze Video Introduction," *DeuzeBlog*, <http://deuze.blogspot.com> accessed March 7, 2009.

Deuze, M. (2005), "Towards Professional Participatory Storytelling in Journalism and Advertising," *First Monday*, 10/7, <http://firstmonday.org/htbin/cgiwrap/bin/ojs/index.php/fm/article /view/1257/1177> accessed June 12, 2009.

Donath, J. S. (1998), "Identity and Deception in the Virtual Community," in M. Smith and P. Kollock (eds), *Communities in Cyberspace*, London: Routledge, 29–59.

Eicher, J. B. (1995), *Dress and Ethnicity: Change Across Space and Time*, Oxford: Berg.

Eicher, J. B. and Roach-Higgins, M. E. (1992), "Definition and Classification of Dress: Implications for Analysis and Gender Roles," in R. Barnes and J. B. Eicher (eds), *Dress and Gender*, Oxford: Berg.

Ellison, N., Steinfield, C., and Lampe, C. (2007), "The Benefits of Facebook 'Friends': Exploring the Relationship Between College Students' Use of Online Social Networks and Social Capital," *Journal of Computer-Mediated Communication*, 12/3, <http://jcmc.indiana.edu/vol12/issue4/ellison.html> accessed November 12, 2007.

Entwistle, J. (2000), *The Fashioned Body: Fashion, Dress and Modern Social Theory*, Cambridge: Polity.

Ess, C. (2002), "Ethical Decision-Making and Internet Research: Recommendations from the AoIR Ethics Working Committee," Association of Internet Research (AoIR), <http://www.aoir.org/reports/ethics.pdf > accessed June 16, 2007.

Etzioni, A. and Etzioni, O. (1999), "Face-to-Face and Computer-Mediated Communities: A Comparative Analysis," *Information Society*, 15/4: 241–8.

Evans, C. (2003), *Fashion at the Edge: Spectacle, Modernity and Deathliness*, New Haven, CT: Yale University Press.

Fiske, J. (1992/2008), "The Cultural Economy of Fandom," in E. Mathijs and X. Mendik (eds), *The Cult Film Reader*, Berkshire: Open University Press McGraw-Hill, 445–55.

Fontana, A. and Frey, J. H., (2003), "The Interview: From Structured Questions to Negotiated Text," in N. K. Denzin and Y. S. Lincoln (eds), *Collecting and Interpreting Qualitative Materials*, London: Sage, 61–75.

Foucault, M., Martin, L. H., and Gutman, H. (1988), *Technologies of the Self: A Seminar with Michel Foucault*, Amherst: University of Massachusetts Press.

France, C., Cahill, J., and Shimazaki, H. (2003), *Cosplay Girls: Japan's Live Animation Heroines*, Tokyo: DH Publishing.

Gallant, L., Boone, M., and Heap, A. (2007), "Five Heuristics of Designing and Evaluating Web-Based Communities," *First Monday*, 12/3, <http://firstmonday.org/htbin/cgiwrap/bin/ojs/index.php/fm/ article/view/1626/1541> accessed November 12, 2007.

Garber, M. (1992), *Vested Interests: Cross-Dressing and Cultural Anxiety*, London: Routledge.

Gauntlett, D. (1997), *Social Theory for Fans of Popular Culture*: *Popular Culture for Fans of Social Theory*, <http://www.theory.org.uk> accessed July 22, 2007.

Gauntlett, D. (2002), *Media, Gender and Identity*: *An Introduction*, Oxfordshire: Routledge.

Gauntlett, D. (2003), *Web.Studies: Rewiring Media Studies for the Digital Age*, Oxford: Arnold and Oxford University Press.

Geertz, C. (1973), *The Interpretations of Cultures*, London: Fontana Press.

Gelder, K. and Thornton, S. (1997), *The Subcultures Reader*, London: Routledge.

Gillham, B. (2000), *Developing a Questionnaire*, London: Continuum.

Glesson, R. (2009), "Culture of Availability," *Deuze Blog*, <http://deuze.blogspot.com> accessed May 7, 2009.

Goffman, E. (1959), *The Presentation of Self in Everyday Life*, Harmondworth: Penguin Books.

Goffman, E. (1972), *Relations in Public*, Harmondworth: Pelican Books.

Gordon, M. M. (1947), "The Concept of a Sub-Culture and Its Application," in M. M. Gordon, *Assimilation in American Life: The Roles of Race, Religion and National Origins*, New York: Oxford University Press.

Gray, J., Sandvoss, C., and Lee Harrington, C. (2007), "Introduction: Why Study Fans?," in J. Gray, C. Sandvoss, and C. Lee Harrington (eds), *Fandom, Identities and Communities in a Mediated World*, New York: New York University Press, 1–18.

Groenewegen, S. J. (1997), "Frocks, Coats and Dress (Non)Sense," in P. Cornell (ed.), *Licence Denied: Rumblings from the "Doctor Who" Underground*, London: Virgin Books.

Gurak, L. J. and Logie, J. (2003), "Internet Protests, from Text to Web," in M. McCaughey and M. D. Ayers (eds), *Cyberactivism: Online Activism in Theory and Practice*, London: Routledge, 25–46.

Hall, S. and Jefferson, T. (1976), *Resistance through Rituals*, London: Hutchinson.

Halperin, D. (1997), *Saint Foucault: Towards a Gay Hagiography*, Oxford: Oxford University Press.

Hebdige, D. (1979), *Subculture: The Meaning of Style*, London: Methuen.

Hesse-Biber, S. N. and Leavy, P. (2006), *Feminist Research Practice: A Primer*, London: Sage.

Hills, M. (2002), *Fan Cultures*, Oxon: Routledge.

Hills, M. (2006), "Not Just Another Powerless Elite? When Media Fans Become Subcultural Celebrities," in S. Holmes and S. Redmond (eds), *Framing Celebrity: New Directions in Celebrity Culture*, Oxon: Routledge.

Hine, C. (2000), *Virtual Ethnography*, London: Sage.

Hodkinson, P. (2002), *Goth: Identity, Style and Subculture*, Oxford: Berg.

Hodkinson, P. (2003), "Net.Goth: Internet Communication and (Sub)cultural Boundaries," in D. Muggleton and R. Weinzierl (eds), *The Post-Subcultures Reader*, London: Berg, 285–98.

Hodkinson, P. (2007a), "Gothic Music and Subculture," in C. Spooner and E. McEvoy (eds), *The Routledge Companion to the Gothic,* Oxon: Routledge.

Hodkinson, P. (2007b), "Interactive Online Journals and Individualisation," *New Media and Society*, 9/4, <http://www.paulhodkinson.co.uk/publications/> accessed June 12, 2008.

Hollander, A. (1997), *Sex and Suits: The Evolution of Modern Dress*, Wilts: Claridge Press.

Hollows, J. (2003), "The Masculinity of Cult," in M. Jancovich, A. L. Reboll, J. Stringer, and A. Willis (eds), *Defining Cult Movies: The Cultural Politics of Oppositional Taste*, Manchester: Manchester University Press, 35–53.

Irwin, J. (1970/1997), "Notes on the Status of the Concept Subculture," in K. Gelder and S. Thornton (eds), *The Subcultures Reader*, London: Routledge, 66–70.

Jenkins, H. (1992), *Textual Poachers*, New York: Routledge.

Jenkins, H. (2006), *Fans, Bloggers and Gamers: Exploring Participatory Culture*, New York: New York University Press.

Jenkins, H. (2008), *Convergence Culture: Where Old and New Media Collide*, New York: New York University Press.

Johnson, D. (2007), "Fan-tagonism: Factions, Institutions, and Constitutive Hegemonies of Fandom," in J. Gray, C. Sandvoss, and C. Lee Harrington (eds), *Fandom: Identities and Communities in the Mediated World*, New York: New York University Press, 285–300.

Joseph-Witham, H. R. (1996), *Star Trek Fans and Costume Art*, Jackson: University Press of Mississippi.

Kendall, L. (1998), "Recontextualizing Cyberspace: Methodological Considerations for Online Research," in S. Jones (ed.), *Doing Internet Research: Critical Issues and Methods for Examining the Net*, London: Sage, 57–74.

King, C.W. (1963), "Fashion Adoption: A Rebuttal to the 'Trickle-Down' Theory," in S.A. Greyser (ed.), *Toward Scientific Marketing*, Chicago: American Marketing Association, 108–25.

Krueger, R.A. (1994), *Focus Groups: A Practical Guide for Applied Research*, London: Sage.

Kunzle, D. (2002), *Fashion and Fetishism: A Social History of the Corset, Tight Lacing and Other Forms of Body-Sculpture in the West*, London: Penguin Social History Classics.

Kunzle, D. (2004), *Fashion and Fetishism: Corsets, Tight-Lacing and other Forms of Body-Sculpture*, Gloucestershire: Sutton.

Lax, S. (2004), "The Internet Democracy," in D. Gauntlett and R. Horsley (eds), *Web Studies*, 2nd ed., London: Edward Arnold, 217–29.

Lievrouw, L.A. and Livingstone, S. (2006), *The Handbook of New Media*, London: Sage.

Lomas, C. (2000), " 'I Know Nothing about Fashion: There's No Point in Interviewing Me': The Use and Value of Oral History to the Fashion Historian," in S. Bruzzi and P. Church Gibson (eds), *Fashion Cultures: Theories, Explorations and Analysis*, London: Routledge, 363–70.

Lull, J. (1988), "The Audience as Nuisance," *Critical Studies in Mass Communication,* 5/3: 239–42.

Lutz, C. (1995), "The Gender of Theory," in R. Behar and D.A. Gordon (eds), *Women Writing Culture*, London: University of California Press, 249–66.

Maanen, J. van (1988), *Tales from the Field: On Writing Ethnography*, Chicago: University of Chicago Press.

MacDonald, A. (1998), "Uncertain Utopia: Science Fiction Media Fandom and Computer Mediated Communication," in C. Harris and A. Alexander (eds), *Theorizing Fandom: Fans, Culture and Identity*, Cresskill: Hampton Press.

Macdonald, M. (1995), *Representing Women: Myths of Femininity in the Popular Media*, London: Hodder Arnold.

Madriz, E. (2003), "Focus Groups in Feminist Research: Rethinking Observation, From Method to Context," in N.K. Denzin and Y.S. Lincoln (eds), *Collecting and Interpreting Qualitative Materials*, London: Sage, 363–88.

Mann, C. and Stewart F. (2000), *Internet Communication and Qualitative Research: A Handbook for Researching Online*, London: Sage.

Marchetti, G. (2008), "Subcultural Studies and the Film Audience: Rethinking the Film Viewing Context," in E. Mathijs and X. Mendik (eds), *The Cult Film Reader*, Berkshire: Open University Press McGraw-Hill, 403–18.

Markham, A. N. (1998), *Life Online: Researching Experience in Virtual Space*, Walnut Creek, CA: AltaMira Press.

Markham, A. N. (2003), "The Methods, Politics, and Ethics of Representation in On-line Ethnography," in N. K. Denzin and Y. S. Lincoln (eds), *The Sage Handbook of Qualitative Research*, 3rd ed., Thousand Oaks, CA: Sage, 793–820.

Marshall, C. and Rossman, G. (1989), *Designing Qualitative Research,* Beverly Hills, CA: Sage.

McCaughey, M. and Ayers, M. D. (2003), "Introduction," in M. McCaughey and M. D. Ayers (eds), *Cyberactivism: Online Activism in Theory and Practice*, London: Routledge, 1–24.

McCracken, G. D. (1992), *Culture and Consumption: New Approaches to the Symbolic Character of Consumer Goods and Activities*, Bloomington: Indiana University Press.

McRobbie, A. (2005), *The Uses of Cultural Studies*, London: Sage.

McRobbie, A. and Garber, J. (1976) "Girls and Subcultures," in S. Hall and T. Jefferson (eds), *Resistance Through Rituals*, London: Hutchinson, 209–22.

McRobbie, A. and Garber J. (1977/1997) "Girls and Subcultures," in K. Gelder and S. Thornton (eds), *The Subcultures Reader,* Oxon: Routledge.

Mellins, M. (2007), "Dressing Up as Vampires: Virtual Vamps: Negotiating Female Identity in Cyberspace," *Networking Knowledge, Journal of MeCCSA PGN*, 1/2, <http://journalhosting.org/meccsapgn/index.php/netknow/article/viewFile/28/66> accessed December 12, 2007.

Mellins, M. (2008), "The Female Vampire Community and Online Social Networks: Virtual Celebrity and Mini Communities," *International Journal of Media and Cultural Politics*, 4/2: 254–8.

Mellins, M. (2010), "Fashioning a Morbid Style: Female Vampire Fans and Subcultural Identity," in B. Cherry, P. Howell, and C. Ruddell (eds), *Twenty-First-Century Gothic*, Newcastle Upon Tyne: Cambridge Scholars.

Michaels, S. and Evans, D. (2002), *The Rocky Horror Picture Show: From Concept to Cult*, London: Sanctuary.

Miles, M. B. and Huberman, M. A. (1994), *Qualitative Data Analysis*, Second Edition, London: Sage.

Morley, D. and Silverstone, R. (1991), "Media Audiences: Communication and Context: Ethnographic Perspectives on the Media Audience," in K. Bruhn Jansen and N. W. Jankowski (eds), *A Handbook of Qualitative Methodology for Mass Communication Research*, London: Routledge, 149–62.

Mullens, L. (2005), "Editor's Introduction," *Spectator* 25/1: 5–10.

Orbach, S. (2009), *Bodies*, London: Profile Books.

Osgerby, B. (2004), *Youth Media*, New York: Routledge.

Paccagnella, L. (1997) "Getting the Seat of Your Pants Dirty: Strategies for Ethnographic Research on Virtual Communities," *Journal of Computer Mediated Communications,* 3/1, <http://jcmc.indiana.edu/vol3/issue1/paccagnella.html> accessed November 12, 2007.

Pallant, J. (2005), *SPSS Survival Manual*, 2nd ed., Berkshire: McGraw-Hill.

Penley, C. (1992), "Feminism, Psychoanalysis and the Study of Popular Culture," in L. Grossberg, T. Nelson, and P. Treicher (eds), *Cultural Studies*, New York: Routledge, 479–500.

Polhemus, T. (1994), *Street Style,* London: Thames and Hudson.

Polhemus, T. (1996), *Style Surfing: What to Wear in the 3rd Millennium*, London: Thames and Hudson.

Porter, D. (1997), "Introduction," in D. Porter (ed.), *Internet Culture*, New York: Routledge, xi–xviii.

Pribham, E.D. (1988), *Female Spectators: Looking at Film and Television*, London: Verso.

Redmond, S. (2006), "Intimate Fame Everywhere," in S. Holmes and S. Redmond (eds), *Framing Celebrity: New Directions in Celebrity Culture*, London: Routledge.

Rosen, C. (2004), "The Age of Egocasting," *The New Atlantis: A Journal of Technology & Society*, 7, <http://www.thenewatlantis.com/archive/7/rosenprint.htm> accessed March 7, 2007.

Sandvoss, C. (2005), *Fans*, Cambridge: Polity.

Short, S. (2006), *Misfit Sisters: Screen Horror as Female Rite of Passage*, Basingstoke: Palgrave Macmillan.

Silverman, D. (2005), *Doing Qualitative Research: A Practical Handbook*, Second Edition, London: Sage.

Silvio, T. (2006), "Informationalized Affect: The Body in Taiwanese Digital Video Puppetry and COSplay," in F. Martin and L. Heinrich (eds), *Embodied Modernities*, Honolulu: University of Hawaii Press, 195–217.

Skal, D. (1992), *The Monster Show: A Cultural History of Horror*, London: Plexus.

Snelson, T. and Jancovich, M. (2009), " 'No Hits, No Runs, Just Terrors': Exhibition, Cultural Distinctions and Cult Audiences at the Rialto Cinema in the 1930s," in R. Maltby, P. Meers, and D. Biltereyst (eds), *The New Cinema History*, Malden, MA: Blackwell.

Spooner, C. (2000), "A Terror of her Robes: Fashioning Gothic Bodies 1789–1999," unpublished PhD thesis, Goldsmiths College, University of London.

Spooner, C. (2004), *Fashioning Gothic Bodies*, Manchester: Manchester University Press.

Spooner, C. (2009), "'Forget Nu Rave, We're into New Grave': Styling Gothic in the Twenty-First Century," Proceedings for the 21st Century Gothic Symposium, January 24, 2008, St. Mary's University College, Middlesex.

Spooner, C. (2010), "Preface," in B. Cherry, P. Howell, and C. Ruddell (eds), *Twenty-First-Century Gothic*, Newcastle Upon Tyne: Cambridge Scholars.

Stacey, J. (1994), *Star Gazing: Hollywood Cinema and Female Spectatorship*, London: Routledge.

Steele, V. (1996), *Fetish: Fashion, Sex & Power*, Oxford: Oxford University Press.

Steele, V. (2001), *The Corset: A Cultural History*, New Haven, CT: Yale University Press.

Steele, V. (2008), *Gothic: Dark Glamour*, New Haven, CT: Yale University Press.

Stern, S. (2008), "Producing Sites, Exploring Identities: Youth Online Authorship," in D. Buckingham (ed.), *Youth, Identity and Digital Media*, Cambridge, MA: MIT Press, 95–117.

Strauss, A. and Corbin, J. (1990), *Qualitative Data Analysis*, Beverly Hills, CA: Sage.

Strauss, A. and Corbin, J. (1998), *Basics of Qualitative Research: Techniques and Procedures for Developing Grounded Theory*, Thousand Oaks, CA: Sage.

Summers, L. (2001), *Bound to Please: A History of the Victorian Corset*, Oxford: Berg.

Tashiro, C. (1996), "The Contradictions of Video Collecting," *Film Quarterly*, 50/2: 11–18.

Telotte, J. P. (1991), *The Cult Film Experience: Beyond All Reason*, Austin: University of Texas Press.

Thornton, S. (1995), *Club Cultures*, Cambridge: Polity.

Thornton, S. (1997), "The Social Logic of Subcultural Capital," in K. Gelder and S. Thornton (eds), *The Subcultures Reader*, London: Routledge.

Tseëlon, E. (1995), *The Masque of Femininity*, London: Sage.

Tseëlon, E. (2001), "Ontological, Epistemological and Methodological Clarifications in Fashion Research: From Critique to Empirical Suggestions," in A. Guy, E. Green, and M. Banim (eds), *Through the Wardrobe: Women Relationship with Clothes*, Oxford: Berg, 237–56.

Turkle, S. (1995), *Life on Screen: Identity in the Age of the Internet*, London: Phoenix.

Turner, G. (2004), *Understanding Celebrity*, London: Sage.

Venters, J. (2009), *Gothic Charm School,* New York: Harper Collins.

Warner, M. (1994), *From the Beast to the Blonde: On Fairy Tales and Their Tellers*, London: Chatto and Windus.

Weber, S. and Mitchell, C. (2008), "Imaging, Keyboarding, and Posting Identities: Young People and New Media Technologies," in D. Buckingham (ed.), *Youth, Identity and Digital Media*, Cambridge, MA: MIT Press, 25–47.

Wester, F. and Jankowski, N. (1991), "The Qualitative Tradition in Social Science Inquiry: Contributions to Mass Communications Research," in K. Jensen and

N. Jankowski (eds), *A Handbook of Qualitative Methodologies for Mass Communi-cation Research*, London: Routledge, 44–74.

Williamson, M. (2001a), "Vampires and Goths: Fandom, Gender and Cult Dress," in W.J.F. Keenan (ed.), *Dressed to Impress: Looking the Part*, Oxford: Berg, 141–58.

Williamson, M. (2001b), "Women and Vampire Fiction: Texts, Fandom and the Con-struction of Identity," unpublished PhD thesis, Goldsmiths College, University of London.

Williamson, M. (2005), *The Lure of the Vampire: Gender, Fiction and Fandom from Bram Stoker to Buffy*, London: Wallflower Press.

Wilson, E. (1985), *Adorned in Dreams*, London: Virago.

Wilson, E. (2003), *Adorned in Dreams, Fashion and Modernity*, Second Edition, London: I. B. Tauris.

Wilson, E. and Ash, J. (1992), *Chic Thrills: A Fashion Reader*, London: Pandora Press.

Winge, T. (2006), "Origins of Anime and Manga Cosplay," in F. Lunning (ed.), *Mech-ademia Volume 1: Emerging Worlds of Anime and Manga*, Minneapolis: University of Minnesota Press.

Winn, J. and Nutt, D. (2001), "From Closet to Wardrobe?," in A. Guy, E. Green, and M. Banim (eds), *Through the Wardrobe: Women's Relationship with Clothes*, Oxford: Berg.

Wolf, N. (1990), *The Beauty Myth: How Images of Beauty Are Used Against Women*, London: Vintage.

Wood, R. (1996), "Burying the Undead," in B.K. Grant (ed.), *The Dread Difference*, Austin: University of Texas Press.

Zoonen, L. van (1994), *Feminist Media Studies*, London: Sage.

Zweerink, A. and Gatson, S. N. (2002), "Cliques, Boundaries, and Hierarchies in an Internet Community," in R.V. Wilcoz and D. Lavery (eds), *Fighting the Forces: What's at Stake in Buffy the Vampire Slayer*, Oxford: Rowman and Littlefield, 239–50.

OTHER RESOURCES

Websites, Forums, and Social Media

Black Waterfall Website, <http://www.blackwaterfall.com/> accessed June 21, 2008.

Brass Goggles Forum, <http://brassgoggles.co.uk/> accessed April 19, 2009.

Chaps.net Website, <http://www.thechap.net/content/section_manifesto/index.html> accessed November 5, 2008.

Dark Angel Design Company, <http://www.thedarkangel.co.uk> accessed June 2, 2007.

Drac-in-a-Box Shop, <http://www.dracinabox.com/> accessed June 2, 2007.

The Dracula Society, <http://www.thedraculasociety.org.uk/> accessed October 21, 2006.

Ebay, <http://www.ebay.co.uk/> accessed June 2, 2007.

Facebook, <http://www.facebook.com/> accessed January 9, 2006.

Gallery Serpentine Shop, <http://www.galleryserpentine.com.au/> accessed April 21, 2009.

Gok Wan's Consumer Website, <http://www.simplygokwan.co.uk/> accessed January 12, 2009.

Gothic Charm School, Episode 1, <http://www.youtube.com/watch?v=mQb4rQm-7_M> accessed February 8, 2012.

Laughing Vampire Shop, <http://www.laughingvampire.com/> accessed February 6, 2007.

LiveJournal, <http://www.livejournal.com> accessed September 1, 2006.

London Vampyre Group Website, <http://www.londonvampyregroup.co.uk/> accessed October 21, 2006.

London Vampire Meetup Group Website, <http://www. vampires.meetup.com> accessed October 21, 2006.

MySpace, <http://www.myspace.com> accessed September 1, 2006.

Net.Goth, <http://www.netgoth.org.uk/> accessed March 16, 2009.

Pandora's Choice: Retro Underwear Shop, <http://www.pandoraschoice.com/> accessed January 12, 2009.

Steamfashion Community, <http://www.community.livejournal.com/steamfashion> accessed April 19, 2009.

SurveyMonkey, <http://www.surveymonkey.com/> accessed Feb. 12, 2007.

Vampyre Connexion Groups Page, <thevampyreconnexion@yahoogroups.co.uk> accessed October 21, 2006.

Vampyre Connexion Website, <http://www.vampyreconnexion.com/> accessed October 21, 2006.

VEIN (Vampire Exchange Information Network) E-mail Group, <vein@vein-europe. demon.co.uk> accessed October 21, 2006.

What Katie Did: Vintage Lingerie Shop <http://www.whatkatiedid.com/> accessed January 12, 2009.

Newspapers/Magazines

Blank, T. (2011), "Giles," *Style.Com*, February 21, <http://www.style.com> accessed April 8, 2011.

Daynes, T. (2006), "E-Goth: Because All Your Friends Live on Your Computer," *Chronicles Magazine*, 2/4: 42–3.

Daynes, T. (2007), "Are We R.O.A.R.ing Loud Enough," *Chronicles Magazine,* 2/7; 42–3.

D'Alessandro, A. (2008), "Vampire Fare Lures Female Viewers: Summit Summons Young Women with 'Twilight,'" *Variety,* November 10.

Kovalic, J. (1997), *Dork Tower Comics (Downloads)*, <http://www.dorktower.com/> accessed February 2, 2009.

Magdalino, V. (2009), "The Edge of Darkness," *ASOS Magazine*, October.

Roby, W. (2008), "Women: It's a Scream," *G2 Magazine,* September 29.

Rosen, M. (1979), "20 Questions Interview," *Playboy*, August.

Sadeian, J. (2008), "Steampunk: What's That All About?," *Chronicles Magazine*, 2/9: 10–11.

Schumann, N. (2006), "Letters Page," *Chronicles Magazine,* 2/6; 39–40.

Schumann, N. (2007), "Letters Page," *Chronicles Magazine,* 2/8; 35–6.

Seifert, C. (2008), "Bite Me (Or Don't)," *Bitch Magazine: Feminist Response to Pop Culture*, December 16, <http://www.bitchmagazine.org> accessed February 2, 2009.

Temple, G. (2007), *Chaps Magazine,* <http://www.thechap.net> accessed April 19, 2009.

Index